HOW
STOP
SMOKING

SIMON MORGAN

Foreword by Sir Richard Bayliss KCVO, MD, FRCP

Virgin

Published by
the Paperback Division of
W.H. ALLEN & Co Plc

A Virgin Book
Published in 1987
by the Paperback Division of
W. H. Allen & Co. Plc
44 Hill Street, London W1X 8LB

Reprinted February 1987 (twice)

Printed and bound in Great Britain by
Anchor Brendon Limited, Tiptree, Essex

ISBN 0 86369 173 0

Design by Sue Walliker

Illustrated by Chris Quayle

CONTENTS

Foreword by Sir Richard Bayliss

	WHAT YOU'RE LETTING YOURSELF IN FOR	7
	DO YOU REALLY WANT TO STOP?	10
Session One	LET'S GET STARTED	19
Session Two	EIGHTY PER CENT THERE ALREADY	49
Session Three	TWO WEEKS TO GO – LET'S GET SERIOUS	71
Session Four	PUTTING IT ALL TOGETHER	87
Session Five	TAKE A DEEP BREATH	111
Session Six	A WEEK WITHOUT SMOKING	139
Session Seven	TIME TO REVIEW PROGRESS	167
	NOTEBOOK PAGES	186

FOREWORD

Although the number of smokers has diminished in recent years, some fifteen million still smoke. And yet many 'thinking' smokers would like to stop. They know it is harmful to their health as the reports from the Royal College of Physicians of London have convincingly shown. Lung cancer, coronary heart disease and respiratory failure due to emphysema and chronic bronchitis take their relentless and avoidable annual toll, particularly of the middle-aged man at the height of his career. But, alas, women too are now catching up.

Apart from its physically lethal effects, smoking is an expensive habit. It is a common cause of fires. It ruins the decoration of your home. It is an annoyance to those who do not smoke. There is nothing to be said in its favour. Yet, knowing all this, people still go on smoking. Many would like to quit the habit. Why don't they?

There are several reasons, but the two main ones are addiction to nicotine and the development of what are called conditioned reflexes. Nicotine is an addictive drug, mainly because of its effect on the brain. Hardened smokers, when they smoke cigarettes with a lower nicotine content, will often smoke *more* to maintain the same nicotine level in their blood as they had before. Nevertheless, many people find it easier to break their addiction to nicotine than to their conditioned reflexes.

Pavlov, the great Russian physiologist who died in 1936, was the first to describe the conditioned reflex. Every time he fed a dog, he rang a bell just before giving it food. After a time the dog would salivate when just the bell was rung but no food was offered. So it is with smokers. They become conditioned to lighting a cigarette when they've had a meal, when they drink a cup of coffee, when they pick up the telephone, when they're writing and can't find the word. Each smoker has his own individual conditioned reflexes, but many of these are common to other smokers.

It is a truism in medicine that when many different forms of treatment are advocated for the cure of a disease, none of them are universally effective. So it is with measures to help people stop smoking. None can claim universal success, but the method advocated in this book has proved as successful, or more successful, than many others. This is because it addresses all the factors that perpetuate the smoking habit. It has been successful for people of all ages, even for those who've smoked for more than fifty years. Certainly you must have at least the wish to stop smoking; you've got this book in your hand. Don't think you haven't got enough will-power (like Mark Twain who wrote, 'It's easy to give up smoking; I've done it thousands of times!') The amount of will-power needed is surprisingly small.

Get going – and good luck. It is so very worthwhile.

Sir Richard Bayliss **KCVO MD FRCP**

WHAT YOU'RE LETTING YOURSELF IN FOR

This book can help *you*.

In it, you'll find a course that will show you how to stop smoking for good. More importantly, the understanding you'll gain on the way will enable you to *enjoy* not smoking.

A tall order, you might think.

If you've ever tried giving up smoking before you might be sceptical of a book that claims that stopping smoking can be easy, let alone enjoyable.

In a way, you'd be right to be sceptical. In this country one in three of us still smoke despite the numerous health warnings and pressures to give up.

There is obviously much more to 'giving up the weed' than simply not buying any more cigarettes.

In my experience the best way of showing someone how to stop smoking is by helping them discover why they smoke and then using that information to help them prepare themselves for a life without cigarettes.

The *HabitBreaker* courses I run are a particularly good environment for this process, the courses all being taught by ex-smokers who stopped smoking on earlier courses.

The book applies the same personal approach that makes the courses so effective.

You may find it odd to have a book 'talk to you', but once you get stuck into the course you will be looking forward to stopping smoking four weeks from now.

But there isn't a magic pill hidden between the pages of any of the chapters. *You* will be doing the work. *I* think you'll enjoy the process as much as the result. And what you stand to gain is enormous.

On average, you'll live five to six years longer, save yourself a fortune, look, smell and feel better as well as gaining self-esteem and confidence as you kick a habit that you know is damaging to you.

Stopping smoking is probably the single most important change you'll ever make to your lifestyle. As a smoker, you've undoubtedly thought about the dangers and you've probably asked yourself a number of times, 'Why on earth do I carry on smoking if I know it isn't doing me any good.'

It's difficult to stop smoking. Not only have you the addiction to nicotine to contend with, smoking has become such a part of your day-to-day existence that even imagining doing without cigarettes is unpleasant. Most people are, at best, *uneasy* at the prospect of 'never smoking again'.

If you have found it difficult to stay off cigarettes in previous attempts you'll enjoy this book. It won't preach at you the dangers of smoking – we all know them. Simply spelling out the risks to health, while making you want to stop, doesn't make the task of stopping smoking, in practical terms, any easier.

What the book *will* do is prepare you both mentally and physically for the most important change to your health that you can make.

You Mean This Might Actually Work?

If you follow the instructions to the letter you'll be astonished at how easy the whole affair can be.

What this book offers is a well-structured programme of things to do and think about that will break down the smoking habits you've built up over the years.

You'll be asked to challenge some of your points of view

about the 'value' of smoking, learn how non-smokers react in situations when you'd normally reach for a cigarette, and find out how to deal with physical problems associated with withdrawal such as weight gain, stress control, and physical cravings.

If you decide to go ahead with the programme you will be asked to devote two hours each week, preferably at the same time each week, for seven consecutive weeks, reading and then acting upon the information given in each of the chapters.

During the weeks between the chapters you will be asked to carry out simple tasks that won't take up much of your time, but will make the 'withdrawal experience' relatively painless.

I'm even insisting *you don't stop smoking until the day after the fifth chapter,* four weeks from now.

By the time you reach the end of the book you'll have not been smoking for two weeks. What's more, you'll have found the desire and the tools you need never to want to smoke again.

But I'm Not Sure I Want To Stop Yet.

You might find yourself saying, 'But I enjoy smoking. I'm not really sure that I want to give it up.'

Sound like you? Here's something to think about.

If there was a magic button that could instantly change you into someone who didn't smoke, wouldn't you press it?

It may not be as mysterious as a magic button, but you should find this programme just as effective. You need to persevere, but you'll probably be surprised at how little will-power you actually need.

Still not convinced that you do want to stop – for good?

THE WHOLE OF THE NEXT SECTION IS DEDICATED TO YOU, THEN.

DO YOU REALLY WANT TO STOP?

Chances are you already know for certain that you want to stop. According to British and American medical opinion at least 70 per cent of smokers want to give up, or have tried to give up smoking before.

Nevertheless, most smokers have doubts about the *strength* of their desire to stop, and may feel that although they *ought* to stop smoking they don't *really* want to.

Obviously, if you are certain that you don't want to stop smoking, then there's not much point even starting the course. Most studies of smoking behaviour have concluded that, beyond all else, *it is the quality of the decision to stop that is the decisive factor*.

Think about it for a moment. If you try and follow the exercises in the book without really being sure that you want to stop, you're bound to find it harder.

So this next section is to help you make that decision.

EXERCISE

Ask yourself the following questions:

	Yes	No
1 Ever wish you'd never taken up smoking?	☐	☐
2 Ever tried giving up before?	☐	☐
3 Ever worry about the risks to your health?	☐	☐
4 Have you changed to a low tar brand, hoping it's safer?	☐	☐
5 Have you ever gone to bed telling yourself that you've smoked your last cigarette – only to have had one by mid-morning the next day?	☐	☐

6 Do you resent spending perhaps £500 per year ruining your health? ☐ ☐

7 Did you buy this book? ☐ ☐

If you have answered yes to any one of these, then underlying whatever else you may feel about smoking, you do have a desire to stop. You wouldn't bother reading this far unless you had a measure of desire to deal with the problem.

Nevertheless, however rational the decision to stop seems, most smokers are not 100 per cent committed to what appears to be a life without one of their main sources of pleasure.

Let's look at the subject another way. Here is another exercise to help you make the decision.

Get a pencil and a watch ready. This is not an exercise to persuade you one way or the other, but to make it easier for you to make your decision. Just spend three minutes, no more and no less, compiling your list of all the good things about smoking.

Time yourself. Start now.

WHAT DOES SMOKING DO FOR ME?

Let me hazard a guess at some of the things you may have written.

I enjoy a good smoke. Do you? What do you mean by this 'enjoyment'?

Can you remember the first cigarette that you ever smoked? Did you 'enjoy' that, or did it make you dizzy and cough?

Anyway, what is so enjoyable about sticking a tube of vegetable matter into your mouth, setting fire to it, and then breathing in poisonous fumes? More about enjoyment later.

It helps me relax. Does it? Smoking INCREASES your heart rate. A smoker's heart beats on average ten thousand times more per day than a non-smoker's. Still relaxed?

It gives me a lift. Yes, it probably does. But you pay for it later – you will feel less energetic a while after the cigarette. Again, I'll explain more later.

It helps me concentrate. Really? Then how do you account for the fact that in memory tests, non-smokers consistently outperform smokers?

One of the constituents of cigarette smoke is carbon monoxide, a poison. Your brain feeds on oxygen – so why should it perform better with carbon monoxide?

If I didn't smoke, I'd put on weight. You don't have to put on weight when you stop smoking. We will show you how not to, but most importantly you must realise that it is *not* not smoking that makes you fat, it is eating out of tune with your bodily needs.

Let's go back to enjoyment for a moment. On the *HabitBreakers* course we suggest that what you call the 'enjoyment' of smoking, is actually little more than the relief of discomfort caused by your addiction to cigarettes in the first place.

In other words you smoke to ease discomfort, rather than for something pleasurable in itself. Some smokers can see this instantly. Others, like myself when I took the *HabitBreaker* course, take quite some persuading.

If you are like me, you might care to ponder the same questions my *HabitBreaker* course leader asked me.

Do you really think that smoking gives you something especially enjoyable, something that non-smokers are missing out on?

Couldn't it be that the 'enjoyment' from cigarettes is only really there because you've become addicted and not having one makes you feel uncomfortable?

For example. Imagine yourself sitting in an aeroplane on the way to your summer holidays. The plane is full. It is hot and stuffy. Because of some problem or other, your plane has now been sitting on the tarmac for an hour. As if that wasn't enough, if the plane doesn't take off soon, you're going to miss the only ferry connection this week.

The 'No Smoking' sign is on.

You didn't have a chance to have a smoke in the lounge before you joined the plane because the queues for Passport Control were heavy. It has been some hours since you last smoked.

Finally, the plane starts to move on the runway, and as it takes off you glance around at your co-passengers in the smoking section, and everyone is waiting, cigarettes in mouths, lighters and matches at the ready.

The plane reaches altitude, the light goes out, you light your cigarette and take a long, deep drag.

HOW DOES THAT FEEL?

Isn't the enjoyment merely the relief of all sorts of uncomfortable sensations caused by not being able to smoke?

Do you *really* think that you have got a pleasure that the

non-smoking passengers have missed out on?

This is the DISCOMFORT THEORY in practice. I suggest that what you have been calling enjoyment is no more than the relief of discomforts caused by being addicted to smoking.

Let's take this idea one step further.

Imagine you are out at a party or other social occasion. You're a little shy because you don't really know anyone there. Do you light up? Are you smoking for enjoyment, or to relieve a feeling of uncomfortableness?

Or imagine you've just got home after a hard day at work. Your partner, for no reason at all, starts arguing with you and it develops into a full-scale row. You light up a cigarette. Is it enjoyable? Or a relief of discomfort?

Can you think of any other times that you light up to relieve discomfort?

By now you should be re-examining some of your views about enjoyment and smoking. Although you may still think that there are certain situations in which smoking is enjoyable, what I'd like you to do is to ask *yourself* just how much enjoyment you get out of every cigarette that you smoke from now on.

What else is good about smoking?

It's good for keeping mosquitoes out of tents; cigarette butts can be strained and used as a spray against aphis on roses; the ash can be used to help restore furniture; and a burning cigarette is still one of the best indicators of light wind direction for sailors.

The question I'd like you to retain uppermost in your mind is – 'What is it that I get out of cigarette smoking that non-smokers are missing?'

It's a pertinent question.

Now let's take a look at some of the *benefits* you could expect if you stopped.

Make a list of all the benefits that you think you would get if you were successful at stopping. Time yourself to spend five minutes on the exercise.

Please try and be specific. Simply writing 'health' as a benefit of not smoking isn't really a lot of use. What do you mean by health? Do you mean that you'd expect better health in the form of more stamina, easier breathing etc, or do you mean that you would reduce the risks of disease? Do you mean both? Be specific.

WHAT WOULD STOPPING SMOKING DO FOR ME?

Let's compare your list with mine.

I've divided the benefits into four categories: health, presentation, inconvenience and self-esteem. Let's take them one by one.

HEALTH

I wouldn't have to worry about lung cancer, emphysema, gangrene, heart attack, high blood pressure.

I would be fitter all round.

My breathing would be clearer.

I wouldn't cough so much.

I wouldn't wake up with a filthy taste in my mouth.

PRESENTATION

My clothes wouldn't smell so much.

I wouldn't have to hesitate before getting close to someone because of my breath.

I wouldn't burn holes in my best sweaters.

My house would smell fresher.

No more nicotine stained fingers.

My singing might be clearer.

INCONVENIENCE

At £1.55 a pack and twenty a day I'd save at least £550 a year.

I would never have to worry about inconveniencing non-smokers.

My husband/wife/kids would stop nagging me.

I would never have to rush out before the pub, late-night shop or garage closes to make sure I have enough for the night.

I wouldn't have to ask for an ashtray again in a non-smoker's house.

I wouldn't have to rush out in intervals at the theatre, cinema, meeting, just for a smoke.

I wouldn't have to send my clothes to the cleaners so often.

SELF-ESTEEM

(For many people this is the most important category.)

I wouldn't be a slave to a habit and a drug.

I wouldn't set a bad example to my kids.

No more 'bumming' cigarettes off relative strangers.

I wouldn't have to worry about the dangers of smoking.

I'd never have to go to bed praying that in the morning I'd wake up a non-smoker.

I'd have finally kicked a habit that has ruled me for most of my adult life.

If I could quit smoking I could do anything.

Quite a lot of benefits. Even if you decide that there is some element of enjoyment in smoking you have to give up an awful lot to get that enjoyment.

Is it worth it?

This past exercise may make it easier for you to decide whether or not to make a serious attempt to stop smoking once and for all.

As I mentioned at the beginning of this chapter, the prospect of actually succeeding at stopping smoking is quite confronting. Although, rationally, it seems obvious which you would prefer – all the benefits of not smoking vastly outweigh the advantages of carrying on smoking – when you come to make your decision you will probably feel a little uncertain.

Is it the right time?

How do I know the course is going to work?

I haven't got enough will-power.

I've tried so many times to stop before and I've never succeeded – why should I now?

I'm still not convinced that I want to stop.

Will I always be thinking about cigarettes?

If you didn't have a number of doubts you would be unusual. After all, if you've smoked for as long as you have, it would be surprising if you didn't have any uncertainty. It's a bit like getting married, or starting a new job; you hope it's going to work out all right, and you are willing to give it your best, but when the day finally arrives you will undoubtedly be a little apprehensive.

It's just about decision time.

We have looked at the advantages and disadvantages of being a smoker. We suggested that you don't actually enjoy all the cigarettes you smoke. You answered a number of questions about your own attitude towards stopping smoking. You may still have some uncertainty, and we'll discuss this again later in the book, but on the bottom line:

Do *you* really want to stop smoking for good?

If you do, then I hope that together we can make the job easier. You'll need the following items. Please get them together as soon as possible.

A pencil small enough to be kept inside a cigarette packet, which we'll call your 'cigarette pencil'.

An elastic band.

A toothbrush, some toothpaste, some dental floss and some mouthwash (any brand that is strong and has an unusual, not minty, flavour).

And a small bag to carry them around with you to work and when you're out.

You'll also need to schedule the seven weekly sessions into your diary.

Lastly, you may want to get some support and do the course with a close friend, relative or even a group. I have found that working in a group is more effective than trying to do the course all by yourself. You will be able to help the rest of your group when their motivation is flagging, and vice versa, and you will also benefit from discussing the concepts together.

If, however, you're still not sure that you want to stop, then DON'T start the rest of the book yet. Wait until you are positive that you do want to.

1

1

SESSION ONE

LET'S GET STARTED

There are seven chapters/sessions for you to read and act on over the next seven weeks.

You won't be asked to stop smoking or to cut down at all until the day after the fifth week. Until that time please smoke as many as you like.

Each session will consist of information about smoking or smoking-related subjects for you to consider. Not all the ideas will apply to everyone, and you may even disagree with some of the points that are made. Please, however, do not reject these ideas out of hand until at least one week has passed.

During the week between each chapter you will be asked to perform some simple tasks and to do a small amount of homework. While you are performing these tasks those ideas that you may originally have rejected may become more acceptable.

While the ideas and information are for you to consider, the assignments that are given to you at the end of each chapter are not.

The assignments are there to make it easy for you to

succeed. If you mess around with them, or choose which ones you think are relevant to you then your own success is in jeopardy right from Day One.

Don't forget that you're about to make the single most important change to your health and lifestyle for a long time. It's worth giving it considerable effort.

When we are teaching the course we tell our students:

'If you think that the assignments are a nuisance, childish or inconvenient you would do well to remember that smoking is definitely a nuisance and inconvenient – and perhaps childish too – and you only have to do the assignments for the next seven weeks!'

The assignments aren't that difficult or complicated, but you will need some self-discipline to complete them satisfactorily.

The focus of this first week is on preparing the paperwork that you will be using to investigate your own unique smoking behaviour, examining some basic assumptions about smoking, agreeing certain ground-rules, and giving you the first week's assignments.

On the next page there are some questions for you to answer about the things that you've had to put up with as a smoker. You will be filling this form in again during the seventh session, to see how much has improved after two weeks not smoking.

WHAT YOU PUT UP WITH

(Please tick yes or no for each item.)	WEEK 1 YES	WEEK 1 NO	WEEK 7 YES	WEEK 7 NO
1 Do you have an annoying persistent cough?				
2 Do you produce phlegm in the morning?				
3 Do you find it necessary to clear your throat frequently?				
4 Do your eyes frequently itch or burn?				
5 Do the membranes of your nose feel parched?				
6 Do you ever have pounding or ringing in your ears?				
7 Do you often have a dry sore throat?				
8 Do you sometimes have a tight, uncomfortable feeling in your chest?				
9 Do you suffer from acid indigestion?				
10 Do you wake up in the morning with a 'dark brown taste' in your mouth?				
11 Does your tongue often feel rough and sore?				
12 Do you become winded very quickly when engaging in physical activities?				
13 Does your breath smell?				
14 Do you hesitate to get too close to anyone because of your smoker's breath?				
15 Do you ever have a slight tremor in the morning?				

16 Do you ever have a cold tingly numbness in your fingers and/or toes?				
17 Do your hands perspire or tremble when you get excited?				
18 Do you ever have a numb pain in your arm?				
19 Do you have frequent headaches?				
20 Does your vision seem to be impaired?				
TOTALS				

Next, some basic information about you and your smoking history.

YOUR PERSONAL PROFILE

Your Name ....

Your Age ....

How old were you when you started smoking? ....

Why did you start smoking? ....

How many do you smoke per weekday? ....

per weekend day? ....

Total smoked per week? ....

Brand you currently smoke ....

Have you ever tried stopping before?
Often   Occasionally   Never

By which methods:
Hypnosis
Acupuncture
5 Day Plan
HabitBreaker Course
Cutting down slowly
Starting later each day
Smoking other people's only
Cold Turkey
New Year's Eve
Illness
Other

What is the longest period that you have stayed off cigarettes?..

Do you feel guilty about smoking? Yes/No

If married, does your spouse smoke? Yes/No

Does he/she object to your smoking? Yes/No/Sometimes

Do your children object? Yes/No/Not applicable

Name any work or social situation in which smoking embarrasses you ....

How much alcohol do you consume in an average week? (Use whatever measures you find easiest.) ....

How many cups of tea and/or coffee do you drink each day? ....

How many other caffeine containing drinks (e.g. coke, pepsi) per day? ....

Have you ever been advised to stop smoking?
By a doctor? ....
Others? ....

How tall are you? ....

How much do you weigh? ....

Do you consider yourself underweight? Yes/No
By how much? ....
overweight? Yes/No
By how much? ....
neither? ....

Finished?

TAKE A BREAK

OK

THE NOTEBOOK

Turn now to your notebook pages at the end of the book.

On the first page in BLOCK CAPITALS you'll see:

I WILL STOP SMOKING ON ....day

(This Cut-Off Day is the day after the fifth session. If you have planned weekly sessions it will be four weeks and one day away.)

Make a note in your diary of the date and plan to celebrate.

PLENTY OF SMOKING TIME LEFT YET, THOUGH.

Next, you'll see that we have divided the notebook into four sections.

The four sections of the notebook are labelled as follows:

1 KEY IDEAS and SESSION NOTES
2 ASSIGNMENTS
3 MAJOR LISTS
4 DIARY

I'll explain each of these sections as we go along.

Consider this notebook as part of your smoking paraphernalia from now on. Carry the book around with you so that you can note discoveries about your smoking behaviour.

The notebook has four purposes.

- Firstly, it is useful for reviewing should the urge to smoke return once the course is over.
  Surprisingly, perhaps, the most often quoted reason for a return to smoking by participants on our courses is complacency.

Should you become complacent at your continued success at being able to stay off cigarettes you might think that you could handle the occasional cigarette. If you remember all the effort that you put into stopping by re-reading your notebook, it may persuade you to think otherwise.

After all, how many times before when you've tried to stop smoking did you think that you could have 'just one?'

- Secondly, the notebook is available for writing down the key ideas in the book and your reaction to them. You may also want to make the occasional note to yourself as you make discoveries about your smoking behaviour in between sessions.
- Thirdly, it will act as a diary of your experiences during the first few weeks after you have smoked your last cigarette. More about this later.
- Lastly, and most importantly for the time being, it will remind you of the correct assignments.

RECORDING YOUR CIGARETTES

Please record and think about each cigarette that you smoke.

Here's how to go about it.

At the back of the book you will find your PACKSTRAP. You will need one of these for each of the first *three* sessions, so photocopy it.

Label the columns with the days of the week starting from today.

Running down the columns are the hours of the day, starting at 5am and finishing at 4am on the following days.

Wrap your packstrap around your cigarette pack with the elastic band. (See diagram.)

WAIT A MOMENT!

If you have got to this stage in the book without having the materials mentioned earlier in this chapter do yourself a favour and stop right now.

If you throw yourself into this programme it will work.

It has worked for thousands of people from all walks of life – in seminar form. One of the advantages of seminars is that they are an environment in which the mere presence of a course leader and a group of other people working towards the same goal produces a certain discipline.

On our courses we ask participants to impose their own discipline and agree to follow our guidelines for success. These include such mundane items as being on time for the meetings, letting the course leader know of any real problems immediately, and making stopping smoking the most important priority in their lives for the weeks that they are on the course.

I don't want to be pushy or too authoritarian but I know from experience that if someone isn't doing the required amount of homework they aren't going to stop smoking.

It's as simple as that.

This stopping smoking business is for *you*. If you follow the course exactly you should not even *want* to smoke anymore.

Isn't that worth going full out for?

The trouble with information being given in book form rather than seminar form is that there is no chance for personal interactions and guidance.

And, *by not having your materials* you are setting yourself up for failure right from Day One.

Please, please follow the instructions.

You don't need a lot of will-power to complete this course. I can think of many people who have obviously got 'will-power' but who have found stopping smoking next to impossible.

Sir Richard Bayliss, who wrote the Foreword to the book, didn't get where he was without 'will-power'. Yet he carried on smoking until he took the *HabitBreaker* course in 1985.

Some Olympic athletes smoke – and yet they probably have more 'will-power' than most of us DREAM of.

You have probably demonstrated that you have will-power in other areas of your life apart from smoking.

There are straightforward techniques that make the process easy for the great majority of people.

1 Please have the materials requested ready.

2 Book your seven weekly sessions into your diary. Treat these sessions as vitally important meetings with yourself, and reschedule only if strictly necessary. *Make succeeding a priority.*

3 Persevere. The methods do work, but there will undoubtedly be times when you feel less positive than others. (I'll talk about self-pity and its effects in Session Two.)

4 Follow the course exactly as it is presented. No chopping or changing the rules to suit yourself.

Enough of the lecture and on with the materials.

Back to the PACKSTRAP.

Wrap it around your cigarette packet with the elastic band. Put your 'cigarette pencil' inside your pack.

Each time you reach for a cigarette the pencil, being heavier than a cigarette, should come out first. Glance at your watch and make a note in the appropriate column on your packstrap each time you light up. (See example.)

	D		D		D		D		RECAP	
AM	5		5				5		5	
	6		6				6		6	
	7		7		7				7	
	8		8		8				8	
	9	|	9		9				9	
	10	|	10		10				10	
	11		11		11				11	
	12		12		12				12	
PM	1	|||	1		1				1	
	2		2		2				2	
	3	|	3		3				3	
	4	|	4		4				4	
	5		5		5				5	
	6	|||	6		6				6	
	7	|	7		7				7	
	8	|	8		8				8	
	9	|	9		9				9	
	10		10		10				10	
	11	||	11		11				11	
	12		12		12				12	
	1		1		1				1	
	2		2		2				2	
	3		3		3				3	
	4		4		4				4	
	T		T		T				T	

Rules about Packstrap

1 Record *every* cigarette that you smoke. Don't forget to mark down cigarettes that you are offered, and remember to make a note later if you smoke somewhere that you are unable to write (in the car for example).

Please try and be as accurate as possible.

2 Keep the packstrap on the outside of the pack – it effectively disposes with millions of pounds worth of cigarette packet design: packs are designed to look attractive, the packstrap is not.

Keeping the packstrap on the outside will also act as a reminder to you to notice your cigarettes more.

3 Smoke as much as you like. Do not deliberately deny yourself cigarettes. By the fifth session you will not only be ready physically to stop smoking; you won't want to smoke. Don't deprive yourself now.

4 Do not total your daily intake or your weekly intake until you sit down at the beginning of the next session.

Next is your RECORD OF CIGARETTES.

Mark today's date next to Session 1.

Head the first row, adjacent to the TOTAL WEEKLY box, with the days of the week starting with today.

Then estimate how many cigarettes, cigars or pipes, that you smoke on each day of the week, and enter your estimate under the days of the week. (Don't worry – I won't hold you to smoking exactly this number.)

At the start of each session you will transfer your packstrap total to the RECORD OF CIGARETTES form.

RECORD OF CIGARETTES

DATE	WK	TOTAL WKLY	DAILY TOTALS						
	1								
	2								
	3								
	4								
	5								
	6								
	7								

PEAK SMOKING TIME (From Packstrap)

PRIMARY	SECONDARY	TERTIARY

WHY DID YOU START SMOKING?

By the end of the week you'll have a pretty clear picture of how many you smoke and when you smoke them. We'll start looking at why you smoke them right now.

To look older?

More sophisticated?

All my friends smoked?

Got me into pubs earlier? (My own 'reason')

To rebel?

To see what it was like?

My doctor suggested I start? (You'd be amazed!)

My lover, husband, dad, mum, grandfather, Great Uncle Bernard offered me one?

Several of these reasons?

A special reason?

Let me ask you something:

Is the reason that you started smoking still the reason you *are* smoking?

Can you remember your *first* cigarette. Did it taste great?

Think about it. Why did you have that first cigarette? Why did you stick with it? (Most of us even had to learn how to inhale!)

For most people:

THE REASON THAT THEY STARTED SMOKING IS NO LONGER TRUE.

You don't want to look any older, do you?

Which is a pretty good place to start a course on stopping smoking.

Write this down as the first KEY IDEA in your notebook:

THE REASON I STARTED SMOKING NO LONGER APPLIES.

So if that's not the reason you smoke, then why do you carry on smoking?

Spend a couple of minutes thinking of all the reasons you smoke and write them down.

REASONS WHY I SMOKE

Perhaps you had some of these reasons.

I suppose it's just habit
I'm addicted to nicotine
I just haven't got the will-power
I just can't imagine life without them
I enjoy it
It gives me a lift when I'm hungry
It helps me relax
I like it after each meal (a cigarette that is)
I smoke to stave off hunger
I smoke when I'm bored
It helps me concentrate
I smoke to calm myself down
I smoke when I'm depressed
I smoke when I'm out at parties enjoying myself
I like the taste

Let me suggest to you another reason underlying all of the ones you've written.

THE REAL REASON THAT YOU CARRY ON SMOKING IS SIMPLY THAT YOU DO NOT KNOW HOW TO STOP AND STAY STOPPED

(That's until now!)

Think about it. Most of the reasons that I have listed in the lower part of the list are contradictory.

People smoke early in the morning to 'get a lift', but when they get tense they smoke to relax.

People smoke at the end of meals when they are full, yet you also find people who smoke to keep their thoughts off eating.

People smoke when they are depressed, lonely or bored. Yet they also find themselves smoking more at parties and social occasions when they are celebrating.

Some cigarettes appear to taste good, others leave your mouth tasting like the bottom of a parrot cage.

Do any of the reasons that *you* smoke seem contradictory?
It would seem that there must be some discrepancy here,

else nicotine is a truly magical drug.

We'll talk more about the physical process that happens when you smoke in more detail later, but just ask yourself again the question:

IS THE REAL REASON THAT I SMOKE SIMPLY THAT I DON'T KNOW HOW TO STOP AND STAY STOPPED?

Even if you have difficulty accepting this idea completely, I'd ask you to write it down as the second KEY IDEA in your notebook.

Let's go back to the reasons *why* you smoke.

Dr Jerome Jaffe, at the third World Conference on Smoking and Health in 1975, talked about smoking as the

COMPULSIVE SMOKING SYNDROME

He said that there were several aspects of the smoking syndrome including:

the *physical addiction* to the drug nicotine, evidenced by a wide range of 'withdrawal symptoms' upon cessation of the drug;

the *psychological* factors comprising of:

automatic cigarettes, i.e. those that leap into your hand simultaneously with a cup of coffee, gin and tonic, beer, telephone etc;

'emotional' cigarettes, accompanying loneliness, boredom, stress, ecstacy, your 'best friend' etc;

the *social and cultural* factors. To a great extent smoking has been encouraged through the mass media, and different brands and accoutrements 'say' something about the smoker.

People also smoke for 'enjoyment', a subject which we discussed at some length in the previous chapter. You'll recall that I suggested that what you call enjoyment from cigarettes is often no more than the relief of discomfort, whether physical or otherwise.

Write this down as an idea:

WHAT I HAVE BEEN CALLING ENJOYMENT MAY BE NO MORE THAN THE RELIEF OF DISCOMFORT.

This week when you are making your note on your packstrap for each cigarette ask yourself why you are smoking it.

See if there is a 'discomfort' which you are relieving. Or was it an automatic cigarette, or an emotional one? Was it because you needed a nicotine fix?

By the way, I meant what I said about being free to smoke as much as you like. Please don't actively try and smoke less. You won't be able to find out whether you really enjoy cigarettes if you don't smoke them.

This is a programme about self-mastery not self-denial.

A couple more ideas to get through:

Lots of people smoke when they have problems.

Yet cigarettes don't solve problems.

And cigarettes are one problem you really don't need.

They may be a convenient distraction, but setting fire to chopped vegetables wrapped in paper and then breathing in the smoke doesn't actually affect the result of many everyday problems.

Yet, if your tyre were to blow out on the motorway, you would probably reach for a cigarette before the jack. (Or before calling the garage.)

It's important to remember this. Smoking does not make anything better. There is nothing special that smoking gives you that non-smokers haven't got, no magical extra charm or effectiveness.

Write that down as the third KEY IDEA:

SMOKING DOES NOT MAKE ANYTHING ANY BETTER.

Is that really true, I hear you say. Surely it does make things better – sometimes.

Decide for yourself over the next week, not now.

While you let some of that sink in, I want to talk about attitude. Your 'attitude' or mental set about the whole stopping smoking process is fundamental to your success.

Whether or not you accept all the ideas in the book or

not is unimportant compared to your own attitude towards stopping smoking.

If you treat it as parting with a best friend, you'll never get over it.

If you treat it as a major piece of emotional surgery, you won't have any fun following the exercises.

But if you treat it as a subject to be mastered, you'll find freedom and much more.

Many people who have stopped smoking have experienced great improvements in their ability to handle other areas of life as well. After all, once you've succeeded you won't ever be able to think of yourself as 'weak-willed'.

Most people's attempts at stopping smoking on their own have resulted in their return to smoking some time later. Most people are not even sure that they can stop smoking. So perhaps this is the one part of the book where you'll have to trust me. I *know* that you can stop smoking – if you really want to. I have seen hundreds of people succeed, few of whom thought that they would.

We used to charge £240 for members of the public to take the course. As you can imagine, most of the people who were willing to consider paying this sum had tried numerous times to stop smoking before, whether by themselves or with other techniques.

If you have failed before you are bound to feel indifferent about your ability to succeed. Before I took the course I had got to the stage where I had given up 'giving up smoking'. Every time I tried I couldn't stop thinking about cigarettes and I remember hearing myself say: *'If it's this bad I'd rather die younger but happier.'*

Taking the course worked for me, much to my surprise. I stopped smoking on 18 February 1983, having smoked since the age of twelve.

Since then I've supervised over sixty courses. We average about a 90 per cent success rate at the eighth week of our courses, yet when we ask who thinks they will succeed, less than 50 per cent of the hands go up.*

It seems that half of the people are terrified that it won't

*Independent research suggests that about 65 per cent of participants on our courses are still not smoking at the end of a year.

work, and half of them are terrified that it will!

What I'm getting at is this. Most people think that stopping smoking has to be about 'giving up' something. I think that stopping smoking is about gaining control over your behaviour, improving your health and saving you a small fortune. I discovered that smoking wasn't that pleasurable, and certainly not worth the risk and cost. What was I 'giving up'?

Your attitude is all important. You can succeed. *It is possible to enjoy life without cigarettes.*

Last thing before we take a short break: *Stopping smoking does make things better.*

Physically your health will improve. Much of the improvement in health occurs very quickly.

For some insurance purposes you are considered a non-smoker after one year off cigarettes. Most of the benefit to your health will be noticed during that first year.

So write down one last KEY IDEA and then get up and stretch yourself, make yourself a cup of tea or something, and then I'll tell you about your assignments this week.

KEY IDEA:

MY BODY WILL RESTORE ITSELF RAPIDLY

Did you want to smoke as soon as I mentioned a break? Have you noticed any automatic cigarettes already?

ASSIGNMENTS Session One

Before we go on to the goodies I've got in store for you this week, I want to remind you of something.

Man wasn't born with a cigarette in his mouth. Tobacco was brought back to Britain in the early 17th century, reputedly by Sir Walter Raleigh. It only became extremely fashionable in the early 20th century, when a cigarette was a necessity for the socialites, and one of few luxuries for the working class.

It had taken a while for smoking to really catch on, as you can see by King James I's comments on the use of the weed:

'Have you not reason then to bee ashamed, and to forebeare this filthie noveltie ... a custome loathsome to the eye,

hateful to the nose, harmefule to the braine, dangerous to the Lungs, and in the blacke stinking fume thereof, neerest resembling the horrible Stigian smoke of the pit that is bottomlesse?'

It was early in the 1950s that it became generally known that smoking was at least partly responsible for a large number of lung cancers and was a contributing factor in many debilitating diseases.

Since that time we have heard more and more about the risks to our health and to the health of others.

Even though we may be hardened addicts ourselves, it is pretty obvious that there really is precious little good about smoking compared to the benefits of stopping. This is the one thing to remember.

The habit of drawing smoke into the lungs for pleasure is on the way out. You are on your way to a healthier, wealthier and more enjoyable life without the smoking habit.

If you've had any history of failed attempts at 'giving up' smoking, try not to be pessimistic and reluctant to have another go. You'll end up doing fewer of the assignments than you would if you're already half convinced you've failed.

The assignments aren't difficult to do at all. But I tell you now, and I'll keep coming back to it, they are what makes it possible for the actual withdrawal period to be relatively calm and comfortable and for you to prepare your mind for its new life without cigarettes.

You are the one who will be benefiting from all the changes. Don't cheat yourself by doing only the assignments.

Can you remember what your first cigarette was like? Were you in love at first taste or was it revolting? Was it nauseating, giddying and choking?

Most people had to *learn* how to smoke, how to inhale without coughing, how to hold a cigarette. Some of us even practised in front of the mirror.

Smoking is not a natural process to man, nor is it a necessary catalyst to any of the body's metabolic changes or an essential item for dealing with day-to-day 20th-century living.

As your body and mind got used to smoking in the first place, now they are getting ready for operating without cigarettes. That's what the assignments are for.

Follow them religiously.

Assignment One

Plan a celebration for yourself for your first day without cigarettes. Arrange to go out for a meal, take the day off work, take a sauna, or a massage. Do something to celebrate your first day of being a non-smoker. (I make sure I celebrate my stopping smoking day every year.)

Assignment Two

Keep an accurate packstrap. Remember that you don't have to deny yourself cigarettes, just make a note of how many you do smoke and at what time.

Also, keep in mind the discomfort theory we discussed earlier, and try to discover exactly what you mean by enjoyment.

Assignment Three

As well as marking down the cigarettes that you smoke on your packstrap, make a note of the times that you have your three main meals each day, and the times that you go to bed and wake up. Do this by marking an O in the hourly column when you have your three main meals, and an X at the times that you go to bed and wake up.

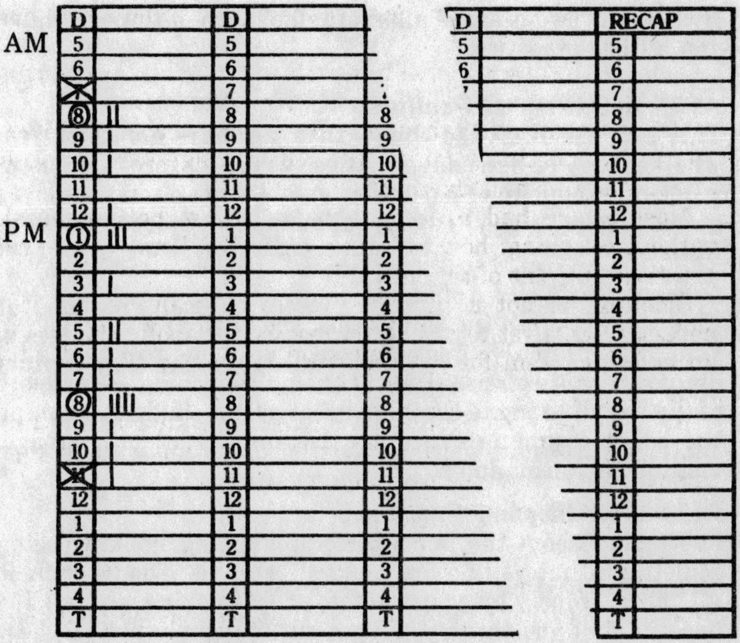

Assignment Four
Observe smokers. Do they seem good-looking and sexy, or slightly haggard, drawn and tense?

Is their attention on the cigarette they are smoking?

Do they look as though they are enjoying their smoking?

Assignment Five
In your notebook there is a section called Major Lists. Head up three sub-sections as follows;

> ASSETS and PERSONAL QUALITIES.
>
> DREAMS, GOALS and AMBITIONS.
>
> REASONS FOR STOPPING SMOKING.

By Session Two prepare a list of ten of each of these. I'll give you a little guidance.

Assets and Personal Qualities
This is a list of all the things that you have going for you, whether they be personal qualities such as a sense of humour, tenacity, kindness, or particular assets that you have such as green fingers, a good education, supportive husband/wife or friends.

Dreams, Goals and Ambitions
This is a list of all the things that you wish to accomplish in your life. Stretch yourself and keep only one foot in reality for part of this exercise. Typical examples include seeing more of the world, living to see one's great grand-children, winning the pools, resuming education, learning another language, visiting the moon and so on.

Reasons for Stopping Smoking
I've talked about the importance of stopping smoking being something that you do for yourself. This list should include all the reasons why you want to stop smoking and all the benefits that you think you'll get out of being a non-smoker.

Come up with ten in each list by next week.

Assignment Six
Taste is a curious thing as far as smoking is concerned. It's the one thing that advertisers of tobacco are allowed to say about their product. I want you to discover what the real taste of cigarettes is this week. Each time that you have a cigarette that 'tastes' particularly good, turn the mark that you made on your packstrap into a 'T' for Taste. (See diagram on previous page.)

Try not to confuse 'relief of discomfort' with taste. Taste occurs in the mouth and nose. Discover how cigarettes taste in your mouth.

Assignment Seven
Change your brand to any other brand that you think you might like.

If you only ever smoke one brand – CHANGE IT. If it makes it any easier, imagine what you would smoke if the company that manufactures your particular brand went out of business – or what brand you would smoke if you booked into a hotel where they didn't sell your brand.

No excuses on this assignment – it's an essential part of breaking your habit. If you're not willing even to change your brand then your chances of succeeding through this course are nil.

If you're not fussy and you smoke two or three brands anyway, choose one that you aren't smoking now, change to it and stick with it all this week.

In either case try to ensure that your new brand has a similar amount of nicotine as your existing brand.

Assignment Eight

Again, if you're serious about making a real effort to stop smoking you won't cheat on this assignment or the next one. They are the most important ones this week.

DELAY SMOKING FOR FIFTEEN MINUTES AFTER YOUR THREE MAIN MEALS OF THE DAY.

If you customarily skip breakfast, then choose which one of your cups of tea or coffee you want to call breakfast and delay smoking for fifteen minutes after it. The same applies for any meal that you miss – have something, even if it is just a glass of orange juice, and then wait fifteen minutes before lighting up.

It should be obvious why we're doing this. Lighting up a cigarette at the end of each meal is probably the most common 'trigger situation'. If you've smoked at the end of every dinner for the last five years or so then your body and mind will be used to the intake of nicotine at that time. We want to break that habit, and so I'm going to ask you to use your own self-discipline to be sensible about this assignment.

If you normally finish dinner and then sit at the table drinking coffee, you have two choices. Either you can wait until after you have had your coffee and then wait fifteen minutes for your cigarette, or you can start your fifteen minutes delay period the moment you finish your last course and have your coffee and cigarette together.

I'll give you some hints as to what to do during the fifteen minutes in the next assignment.

DO NOT CHEAT ON THIS ASSIGNMENT EVEN WHEN IT SEEMS DIFFICULT.

You are capable of not smoking for fifteen minutes. I don't care if you smoke four together after the fifteen minutes is up, but DO NOT SMOKE FOR FIFTEEN MINUTES AFTER YOUR MEALS.

If you don't do this assignment correctly you might as well give up the course now. Sorry to be so brutal about it, but that's the truth. This is an easy assignment – all you have to do is not stick tubes of vegetables into your mouth for fifteen minutes after each meal. If you don't take this exercise seriously, you have already decided that you don't want to succeed as far as I'm concerned.

Even if you're out at a restaurant and it is uncomfortable waiting for fifteen minutes while others smoke – DON'T SMOKE. (It will get easier!)

Assignment Nine

When you smoke you give your mouth a lot of attention. An average of ten drags per cigarette and twenty cigarettes each day means about two hundred drags a day or 73,000 drags a year.

If you stop smoking 'cold-turkey', your mouth will miss the attention and you'll probably replace the attention by eating mints, more mints, more sweets and even more mints. You'll put on weight fast.

Weight is discussed in more detail later on in the book, but many people will recognise that they do need to give their mouths attention.

Remember the toothbrush, toothpaste, dental floss and mouthwash I asked you to have ready? Assignment Nine is to brush your teeth tenderly, lovingly and longingly after each meal (during the fifteen-minute delay time).

When you have brushed your teeth, wash your mouth out with pure undiluted mouthwash. *Do not drink it.*

Also brush your teeth, and use the mouthwash after getting up in the morning and before going to bed. And twice a day, when you feel like it, floss your teeth. Your dentist will love you.

DO take your 'Oral Gratification Pack' with you to work

and use it even at social lunches or dinners. It doesn't have to be embarrassing to brush your teeth in a restaurant – if your dentist instructed you to do so to save your teeth you would find a way to do it.

So FIVE TIMES A DAY you will be brushing your teeth and washing your mouth out with mouthwash. (If you wear dentures then find a soft brush and give your mouth a similar amount of attention.)

Assignment Ten

Do this assignment even if it feels childish or silly. It's effective at programming you to be ready for stopping.

Repeat to yourself every night before going to sleep:

I WILL STOP SMOKING

I WILL LOOK BETTER

I WILL FEEL BETTER

I WILL BE FREE.

(If it makes it any easier, you can add a 'Hallelujah' at the end.)

That's all for the assignments this week. It may seem a lot at first sight, but it doesn't really take much time, and it will make life a lot easier in four weeks' time when you finally put out your last cigarette.

Let's review the first session, and the most important information.

- Firstly, it's important to want to stop smoking for yourself. If you don't want to stop it's going to be a struggle and a process of self-denial. If you do want to then it can be a voyage of discovery leading to a gaining in personal power and self-esteem.
- The reason that you started smoking is no longer true.
- The real reason why you smoke is probably that until now you haven't known how to stop and not start up again.
- You may be confusing 'enjoyment' with relief of discomfort.
- Smoking doesn't make anything better. Smokers don't

have any extra charm, ability or any other qualifications that non-smokers don't have.

- Your body will restore itself rapidly.
- A positive attitude will pay off. You can stop smoking. Millions of people have.

One last thing before you get on with this week's assignments.

It's very easy to lose heart when you don't have much support. If you can follow the exercises in the book with a friend you may well find it easier.

Have a good week and

GOOD LUCK!

2

2

SESSION TWO

EIGHTY PER CENT THERE ALREADY

Hello there! How are you getting on with the assignments? Ninety per cent or better?

Seventy per cent or thereabouts?

Start this session by adding up the number of cigarettes that you smoked this week.

Add the totals both horizontally and vertically on your packstrap so that not only do you get daily totals but you will be able to see which hours of the day you tend to smoke most.

Now transfer the daily and weekly totals onto your RECORD OF CIGARETTES on Page 33. I'll show you how we fill in the Peak Period Section later in this session.

Have your second packstrap ready and wrap it round your cigarette packet. Mark any cigarettes you smoke during this session on your new packstrap.

HOW DID YOU GET ON?

You're certain to be in one of the following three categories!

1 You smoked less than you thought that you would.

2 You smoked more than you thought you would.

3 You smoked about the same amount.

It doesn't matter at all *which* category you are in. At this stage it is unimportant how *many* you smoke; indeed I have seen people on the courses go into the final week still smoking more than 40 a day.

If you smoked less than you thought you would it could be because you have been more aware of each cigarette and some of the 'automatic cigarettes' have gone already. Don't worry if your intake goes up this week, now that some of the novelty has worn off.

If you smoked more than you thought, then you may have been fooling yourself before. Perhaps knowing how many you do smoke will reinforce your determination to succeed. Be that as it may, don't worry and especially don't TRY to cut down at all. Just carry on noticing your habits and every cigarette that you smoke and ask yourself whether or not you really want it.

If you do want it, then have it. (Assuming it's within the rules, obviously.)

As you know, nicotine addiction is one of the main factors of our 'compulsive smoking' syndrome. Different people react differently to withdrawal from nicotine. Some people find that their alcohol tolerance drops, at least for a while. Not only will you save on cigarette costs! Others notice few side-effects of the removal of nicotine from their systems, merely finding the process slightly uncomfortable for a while. A very few people have pronounced effects.

It is obviously a good idea to detoxify the system and make the physical change a gradual one. After all, you may have spent most of your adult life being stimulated by this drug and a gradual change will give your body a decent chance of surviving intact the change-over to normal functioning.

You'll probably find that the number of cigarettes you're smoking will fall off quite naturally at some time in the course. I think the fall often comes when you decide that you don't really want cigarettes anymore. That may not be until the fourth week, though.

Here's how we will be expecting your nicotine intake to change throughout the course.

Let's take an average smoker of 20 middle tar cigarettes per day. Before he/she started on the course he estimated he smoked 20 a day.*

He takes in 1.4 mg of nicotine per cigarette. At 20 a day that's 28 mg of nicotine per day. By the time he's at his fifth session, we would have expected his intake to have dropped by about a third in numbers of cigarettes – down from 20 to 12 a day.

But as he's been slowly weaning himself onto weaker cigarettes and during his last week of smoking is on the lowest available nicotine cigarettes, say with 0.3 mg, his nicotine intake will have dropped even more.

Twelve times 0.3 mg is a total of 3.6 mg per day. From 28 mg a day that's a drop of about 85 per cent. Most people achieve a similar reduction in level.

There are assignments this week for you that will help reduce the nicotine even further. The day before you put out your last cigarette we'll calculate exactly how much *your* nicotine intake has fallen.

In the meanwhile don't try too hard to reduce the amount you're smoking. You won't get a chance to truly discover that cigarettes *aren't* really enjoyable if you feel guilty about every one you smoke.

In fact, smoke as guilt-free as you can. Guilt, as far as I can see, is of absolutely no benefit at all to someone wanting a life of freedom from cigarettes. Wanting to stop smoking is much more powerful than feeling guilty about it.

Let's talk a bit more about nicotine. There is still an immense amount of discussion about the physiological effects of this substance. We know that it makes the heart beat faster. Hormones are released causing a stimulating effect, an increase in your heart rate and the volume of blood pumped out from the heart. High blood pressure is a common

*For my own ease I have used the masculine gender throughout the book. For he please read he or she.

complaint among smokers.

It also appears that nicotine can cause paradoxical effects on different parts of the brain, appearing to stimulate and to relax different areas at the same time.

Nicotine can also affect the stomach and intestines, and it can help addicted smokers concentrate.

It's important to keep the effects of nicotine in perspective. The fact that a drug may make it easier for you to relax in some way or another does not justify a one-in-five chance of contracting a disease related to smoking. The two-thirds of our population who are non-smokers do not need nicotine to relax or to assist any of their daily routines.

While nicotine does seem to help *addicted* smokers concentrate and may help *them* in stressful circumstances, *it does not give them any extra ability that non-smokers don't have.*

As far as you are concerned, this means that you might have temporary difficulties concentrating or relaxing while you are getting used to becoming a non-smoker.

But when you've become accustomed to it your mental abilities could improve.

WHAT'S YOUR HABIT LIKE?

Last week we looked at what smoking was causing you to put up with physically; this week you will see what you have to put up with in a more social context.

Just answer the following questions.

	YES	SOME TIMES	NO
1 Do you smoke before breakfast?			
2 Do you ever wake up during the night just for a smoke?			
3 If you wake up during the night, must you have a smoke?			
4 Do you smoke between courses of a meal?			
5 Do you smoke immediately after each meal?			

6 Do you smoke while riding in a car?			
7 Do you take a 'smoke break' during a sports activity?			
8 Do you carry cigarettes with you at all times?			
9 Do you buy cigarettes by the carton?			
10 Do you smoke while talking on the telephone?			
11 Do you smoke a low tar/nicotine brand because of safety?			
12 Did you ever routinely promise yourself you'd quit smoking?			
13 Are you uncomfortable at lectures, movies, plays, public buildings, etc, where smoking is forbidden?			
14 If there is an intermission at a performance, do you go out for a smoke?			
15 Do you ever 'hate yourself' when lighting up?			
16 Do you ever infringe a 'No Smoking' sign?			
17 While riding in a car on a lengthy trip with non-smokers, do you smoke in spite of their protest and discomfort?			
18 Are you uncomfortable if you're the only smoker in a group?			
19 Is smoking the last thing you do each night?			
20 Did you ever wish that you would wake up one day, free of the habit, and never want to smoke again?			

21 Do you smoke each cigarette to the bitter end?			
22 Would you panic if you were caught without cigarettes for more than two hours?			
23 Do you inhale deeply, so that you feel the smoke in your lungs?			
24 Do you ever feel like lighting up straight after finishing a cigarette?			
25 Do you ever light a cigarette with the one prior to it?			

All that hassle for this illusion of enjoyment?

Is it really worth it?

Now let's go back to last week's assignments. Mark yourself out of ten for how well you did on each one.

Assignment One
Plan your Cut-Off Day celebration.

Assignments Two and Three
How accurate is your packstrap? Are you having three meals a day? Did you mark down the times of awakening and retiring?

Assignment Four
Ten Assets . . . ? Ten Dreams . . . ? Ten Reasons . . . ?

Assignment Five
What did you notice about smokers? Are they calmer, cooler and more collected, or nervous and not relaxed?

Do they look handsome, sexy and virile, or pale, wrinkled and unattractive?

Do they look as though they are enjoying their cigarettes, or are they even aware of the fact that they are smoking?

Assignment Six
Taste. How many 'T's for taste did you have? How many is that compared to the total number of cigarettes that you smoked this week?

Do you think that the taste of cigarettes is a major factor in your smoking habit?

If you did have any 'T's were they after long periods of not smoking? In that case are you sure that you aren't confusing taste with 'relief of discomfort' caused by lack of nicotine in the system?

Or were the 'T's after each meal, when again there was perhaps some relief of discomfort when you were finally allowed to smoke after your fifteen minute delay period?

How many did you note down?

During the courses we normally see about fifteen 'T's from a group of twenty smokers. Assuming that they smoke about twenty a day, that's fifteen cigarettes that tasted good out of two thousand eight hundred smoked in that week.

Of course you might say, 'Well, they simply forgot – if they were smoking the old brand they would have more.'

Are there in fact many less cigarettes that tasted good than you thought? How many 'T's did you mark down *before* you had time to change to your new brand?

Is 'taste' one of the key reasons that you are smoking?

Let's take a close look at any 'T's you may have marked. (Do this exercise again next week if you didn't give much attention to it last week.)

If you have 'T's either first thing in the morning or after meals, you are probably confusing 'taste' with relief of discomfort or 'satisfaction'. It takes 7.5 seconds for the nicotine in the first puff to hit your brain.

Did the cigarette taste good all the way to the filter, or were the first couple of puffs more tasty?

Apples don't taste any different the whole apple through!

Can you remember your first cigarette? Did *it* taste good?

The point of this exercise is to help you be clear about what you are giving up. It doesn't matter if, having done the experiment, you still think that some cigarettes taste good. My mother used to like eating coal when she was pregnant!

What is important is that you aren't left with vague notions as to the value of smoking. It is unlikely that you enjoy the taste of all the cigarettes that you smoke, and it is useful for you to question what you mean by taste in the same way as you are questioning what 'enjoyment' means.

Carry on with this assignment this next week. Try and be exact as to what you like about the taste, and separate the 'desire for' from the 'taste of' cigarettes.

Assignment Seven
Did you change your brand? What was that like? Did you get used to the brand fairly quickly or not?

Assignment Eight
The delay times. Did you manage this 100 per cent of the time?

Did you miss one or two periods through forgetfulness?

Did the fifteen minutes sometimes seem like forever and yet other times thirty minutes or so passed with no real hardship?

What made the difference between the easy times and the more difficult times?

Getting on with something else perhaps? Immersing yourself in conversation or some other activity?

What made it difficult – clock-watching?

Assignment Nine
Your oral gratification routine. Again, judge yourself on how

well you did. Are you beginning to like your mouthwash?

Assignment Ten
Your recitation? Did you do it, or did it get dismissed from your mind?

The pass mark for the assignments over all is 90 per cent.

If you have fallen below 90 per cent on the delay times and on the oral gratification then you are on target for making life difficult for yourself unless you improve.

It isn't easy to keep your commitment up, I know.

And believe me, I do know. I was one of those people who regularly went to bed promising myself that I wouldn't smoke anymore. Yet, time after time, I'd find myself agonising over my 'stupid promise' by mid-morning, and abandoning it completely by lunchtime.

I heard myself say, I'll give up giving up – and if I do die five or six years earlier, at least I'll die happy.

It is difficult to get your mind to accept that there could be enjoyable or even preferable 'life without cigarettes', and that 'giving up smoking' doesn't have to be the saga of failure after failure, causing even the most objective of us to begin losing confidence.

If we have repeated this pattern of trying to stop smoking followed shortly thereafter by taking the habit up again, gradually we come to believe that we can't stop smoking.

We become afraid that we aren't strong-willed enough, a mental state that is reinforced by starting out with the best of intentions followed by a gradual weakening of resolve and eventual resumption of the habit.

You don't have to stop smoking. It is much better to *want* to stop smoking than to *have* to. I much prefer doing things I want to do, rather than things I ought to.

If you have to or you think you ought to but don't really want to, you will always think of not smoking in terms of giving up something.

Dr Fredrickson, of the New York Board of Health, said this:

'As we see it, there are two attitude postures one can opt for during withdrawal. One is negative and basically self-defeating. The other is positive and can be powerfully self-reinforcing.

'When the smoker opts for the self-defeating attitude, he

tends to view withdrawal as an exercise of self-denial. He considers that an object of great value is being taken from him . . . one that may be a source of pleasure or a requirement for normal functioning. He feels that he is being "put upon" being asked to suffer. Inevitably he feels sorry for himself . . . he suffers. This suffering becomes intense. The more he suffers, the greater is the desire to smoke, which in turn intensifies the suffering. This cycle usually results in the generation of intense negative effect that may prove too painful to tolerate.

'And the first excuse that presents itself, he uses to relieve his discomfort.

[Does that remind you of anyone you know?]

'When the smoker opts for the positive, "Of course I can do it" attitude instead, he looks upon withdrawal as an exercise in self-mastery. Rather than taking something away, he is adding to his life – a new dimension of self-control. He is teaching himself a more positive, constructive, self-fulfilling way to behave. There is evidence that for some, development of control over cigarette smoking tends to generalise to other areas of behaviour, bringing in turn, a renewed sense of one's abilities, and often, what appears as an actual increase in one's capacity to deal more constructively with other "Problems of Living".

'Smokers must learn to identify and modify their self-defeating attitudes. . . .'

Which is all very well. But how do you go about doing it?

An Australian psychologist suggests a very simple and effective technique.

He points out that there are two elements to whatever sort of situation you are in: there are its physical attributes, where you are and what's going on; and there are mental attributes, your views, opinions and judgements of your situation and circumstance.

He calls this the

CURRENT VIEW OF THE SITUATION or **CVS**

While the physical attributes of the situation may remain unchanged, you can change your mind. Your opinions and viewpoints can shift, by looking at the situation in a different light.

He says that there is always a **BVS** where there is a **CVS**

BVS stands for BETTER VIEW OF THE SITUATION.

No matter what the situation is, even if it is an extremely good one or just an uncomfortable set of circumstances, there is, if you look for it, a Better View of the Situation.

This is very simple really. I'm just putting down on paper the way that a healthy mind recovers from any sort of unhappy incident. After getting over the direct impact of the incident we start to look for what we've learnt, or what could have been worse, and we put the old problem into a new perspective.

This psychologist's extremely simple exercise consists of repeating to yourself, out loud, one hundred times in quick succession each day:

CVS to BVS

It takes about a minute and thirty seconds if you're quick.

It won't be long before you find yourself in the middle of a really tight, uncomfortable situation thinking all of a sudden:

CVS to BVS

You've got to be kidding! See what happens! This week try this exercise. Repeat to yourself **CVS to BVS** one hundred times in quick succession, at least once a day.

Let's go back to the assignments for a moment. We started this conversation about self-defeating attitudes by discussing how well you did the assignments. You probably didn't do them as well as you could have. (If you did, please excuse me!)

The information that you are being given in this book is all very useful, and I hope that you enjoy reading it. But you will not benefit fully from an understanding of what is being said if you leave out any of the exercises.

If you didn't do 85 per cent of both the delay times and the oral gratification, then you should seriously examine whether you want to succeed. That isn't to say that if you have fouled up much of last week's homework you *can't* succeed, just that you must pay particular attention in the following weeks.

Werner Erhard said something that I thought was useful when making the assignments on the course a priority:

'You can either have what you want, or all your reasons for not having it.'

On the courses we spend much of our time trying to ensure people do assignments to standard. It helps on the courses if the participants have some money to lose if they don't succeed. That usually keeps them doing the assignments even when it would be easier to ignore them.

The assignments get more difficult as we go on, though you only have to do the ones related to smoking for another three weeks now. Surely it's worth the extra effort to really make the best of it.

I can't recommend highly enough the need to do the assignments 100 per cent. Agreed?

Funnily enough, if you did make some attempt at the homework last week you're probably further on the road to stopping smoking than you think. It probably doesn't feel like it, though.

First of all, making your decision to stop gets you half of the way there.

Then there are the automatic cigarettes. I doubt that too many cigarettes found their way into your mouth unconsciously this week. A couple perhaps, but in general you should have been aware of each cigarette that you smoked.

We'll keep on breaking 'trigger' mechanisms that send you reaching for a cigarette as the course progresses.

The physical addiction is being reduced as we've already explained earlier.

I'm sure that you realise now that not smoking is now the social norm.

That's about 80 per cent towards our goal.

What remains are the emotional cigarettes – the cigarettes that you smoke when you're upset or angry, and when you're thrilled.

As we've said before, cigarettes don't make anything better. They may act as a distraction to the problems that you are facing but they don't do anything to solve them. Non-smokers don't have cigarettes to fall back on in the face of a problem, so they either distract themselves in other ways, or get on with dealing with their problems right away.

I would like you to look out for your 'emotional' cigarettes this week, and see whether or not they do affect the outcome of any problem. See if you can think how a non-smoker would have dealt with the same problem.

Perhaps remember your **CVS** to **BVS**.

HOW MUCH DOES SMOKING REALLY COST YOU?

Cigarettes are only part of the cost involved in smoking. There are a large number of hidden costs, from matches, lighters to extra time off work due to being sick (smokers have, on average, five more days off sick than do non-smokers).

Some people have had minor car scrapes due to the unfortunate placing of cigarette butts; there are also burnt clothes, burnt furniture, extra mints and breath fresheners to consider too.

On the HABIT MAINTENANCE COSTS form overleaf, estimate your hidden cost of smoking. Simply hazard a guess at how much any item in the categories might cost you over a year. Then total up the column and divide by twelve to get your MONTHLY MAINTENANCE COST.

HABIT MAINTENANCE COSTS

In addition to the cost of cigarettes, there is a *hidden cost of smoking*. Most smokers consider only the cost of a pack of cigarettes, but that's actually only a *part* of the money that goes up in smoke!

Take a moment to estimate *your own* expenditures in the categories listed below. Add the item costs, then divide the total by 12 to obtain your average maintenance cost per month.

	£
Income lost due to illness caused by smoking (National Average 5 days)	
Car scrapes due to smoking (£50 excess)	
Burned clothing due to smoking	
Burned carpets and furniture	
Breath fresheners, mints, matches, etc	
Additional dental care (20 per cent)	
Additional medical treatment & prescriptions	
Extra dry cleaning – clothing, curtains, etc	
More frequent house, car & office cleaning	
More cleaning products, air sprays, wear & tear	
Repainting home/office more frequently	
Extra mileage driving to the shop for a pack	
Estimated higher cost of Life Insurance	
Maintenance cost per year	
Maintenance cost per month (cost per year ÷ 12)	

HABIT MAINTENANCE FORM

Now let's see how much you spend on cigarettes.

1 How much does your normal pack cost you?______

2 How many packs do you smoke during a month?____

3 Multiply 1 by 2 to get your monthly cost.________

4 Multiply 3 by 12 to get your yearly cost.______

Now add your yearly cigarette cost to your yearly maintenance cost to find out the *real* total yearly smoking cost.

As a guideline, if you are a smoker of 20 a day you will be looking at a total yearly cost of between £600 and £1200.

A lot of money up in smoke.

When you consider that you have to earn the money first and that you pay Her Majesty's Government 30 per cent tax before you have the money to spend, you'll be saving about £1000 a year.

Is it really worth it?

Can you think of things you'd rather spend the money on?

PEAK SMOKING PERIODS

On your RECORD OF CIGARETTES on Page 33 you will see that there is space for you to mark in your peak smoking periods each week.

The purpose of doing this is for you to see clearly when your heaviest smoking periods are, and to understand why they occur.

In the recap column of your packstrap you should have totalled the number of cigarettes that you smoked for each hour of the day.

Look down the column and see if you can identify three main periods this week.

Obviously, we've only got one week's reporting to go on, and so we'll simply find out when the periods are this week, and comment further next week.

BREATHING PROPERLY

When I was at school we had PT twice a week. Our teacher (who had muscles in places where we didn't even have places) instructed us on posture, emphasising the need to stick the chest out.

If you watch a small child breathing when relaxed you will see the stomach rising, rather than the chest.

Funnily enough, you may only be breathing correctly when you are taking a deep drag on a cigarette. Cast your mind back to that aeroplane lifting off the runway.

As the plane approaches a safe height, the non-smoking light goes out, and simultaneously twenty cigarettes are lit.

Twenty deep breaths. Probably the sheer depth of the breath helps the smoker to relax, never mind the effect of the nicotine.

Some of the 'enjoyment' or 'satisfaction' that smokers get is a physical sensation of relief in the stomach region, or more precisely the diaphragm.

Please start examining your own breathing, and as an assignment this week, and for each week that you are on the course, I would like you to perform the following breathing exercise three times a day.

BREATHING EXERCISE

1 Stand up, and slowly breathe out all of the air in your chest. To help force all of the air out, when you think you have breathed out all that you can, try yelling 'Help'. It's surprisingly effective.

2 Place your hands either side of your midline, just below your ribs, and feel your diaphragm moving as you breathe in.

3 Breathe in slowly and steadily, forcing your diaphragm out.

4 Breathe out again as in 1.

Repeat the breathing exercise three times, three times each day. You will find it invaluable later on.

ASSIGNMENTS Session Two

So now we come to the assignments for the second week. They aren't really much more difficult than last week.

Assignment One
Continue oral gratification.

Assignment Two
Continue searching for taste.

Assignment Three
Continue observing smokers.

Assignment Four
Continue recording your cigarettes on your packstrap, but this week mark down every time you have a cup of tea or coffee with a 'C', and every time you have a glass of alcohol mark the packstrap with an 'A'.

	D		D				D		RECAP	
AM	5		5				5		5	
	6		6				6		6	
	7		7		7		7		7	
	8	IC	8		8				8	
	9		9		9				9	
	10	I	10		10				10	
	11	IC	11		11				11	
	12		12		12				12	
PM	1	IAIA	1		1				1	
	2	IAII	2		2				2	
	3		3		3				3	
	4	ICII	4		4				4	
	5		5		5				5	
	6	ICIC	6		6				6	
	7	IAIIIA	7		7				7	
	8	IA	8		8				8	
	9	II	9		9				9	
	10		10		10				10	
	11	IC	11		11				11	
	12		12		12				12	
	1		1		1				1	
	2		2		2				2	
	3		3		3				3	
	4		4		4				4	
	T		T		T				T	

Assignment Five
Continue your night-time recitation. I will stop smoking, I will look better, I will feel better, I will be free.

Assignment Six
Change your brand to one that you dislike. It's not necessary to change the type of tobacco from Virginia to French, or from normal to menthol (or vice versa) but do smoke a cigarette you dislike.

Assignment Seven
Change the dominant hand and side of mouth that you smoke with.

Does that affect the 'enjoyment' of the cigarette? Try and smoke in the unusual hand all this week.

Assignment Eight
Change the location of your cigarettes from the place where you usually keep them, your handbag, jacket pocket etc, to somewhere unusual – not necessarily inconvenient.

Assignment Nine
Get rid of all your smoking paraphernalia, your favourite lighters, ashtrays, cigarette cases, and put them away in the attic for sale in the next century as antiques.

Assignment Ten

Increase the delay times after each meal to thirty minutes. That's thirty minutes after three meals a day. You should start eating something for breakfast if you can.

Assignment Eleven
Don't smoke for ten minutes after a cup of tea or coffee.

Assignment Twelve
Don't smoke for ten minutes after alcoholic beverages.

Please note. Once again, I urge you to complete the assignments as well as you are able, particularly the delay times. Try and use your imagination to get over difficult moments, and avoid self-pity at all costs.

A short review of the session!

- Stopping smoking is a personal experience, not something anyone can do for you.
- You can stop smoking by sticking to the assignments and by re-examining your attitudes towards smoking as we discuss them. In fact, if you've made a decent stab at the first week's assignments, you're well on the way already.
- I went on and on about the assignments.
- We discussed the true cost of smoking.
- We talked about nicotine addiction, and how yours will be reduced.
- We discussed taste.
- I brought up the subject of attitude again, and introduced you to the **CVS** to **BVS** exercise.
- You learnt a new breathing exericse.
- And you have another set of assignments for the coming week.
- Enjoy yourself.

3

3

SESSION THREE

TWO WEEKS TO GO – LET'S GET SERIOUS!

I'm assuming that having got this far into the book and the course you're treating it and yourself seriously. In other words, you are following the assignments now.

I might be wrong.

As course instructors we consider it one of the main parts of our job to encourage and exhort our would be non-smokers to do the assignments as well as possible.

It is almost inevitable that at some stage you will find some of the assignments difficult.

It is also inevitable that as the course progresses your motivation will change, from being highly positive and confident one moment to questioning whether or not you actually want to stop smoking at all.

Many people who join in the courses start asking us at this stage whether or not they 'couldn't just stop now'. Having completed the assignments so far they find that they are ready for stopping and they don't want to wait any longer.

Others feel differently, and having started off slowly with the assignments wish they could have an extra week or so.

So I thought that we would start this third session by talking about the different attitudes that are common at this stage in the proceedings. If you are finding either that the assignments are proving difficult, or if your commitment and motivation are wavering from time to time you might find comfort from the fact that many others have felt the same way.

To their own surprise the great majority of them succeed.

It is still totally natural to be sceptical, anxious and worried that you're going to fail and are wasting your time and energy.

It is totally normal to be feeling frustrated and even upset with yourself if you haven't been completing the assignments as well as you would like to have done.

You have still got two weeks to go.

Keep reminding yourself that stopping smoking really is one of the most important things in your life. That in two weeks time you will be kicking a habit that has probably had you in its stranglehold all your adult life.

This week the assignments get serious. If you have frequently been cheating yourself over the half-hour delay times you have got to make a decision as to whether you wish to continue the course or not.

It is pointless carrying on if you are not going to give it 100 per cent from now on. There's no point in simply reinforcing your history of past failed attempts.

If you are having severe problems sticking to the assignments, say less than 75 per cent until now, then it may be that now isn't the right time for you to stop.

Don't use that as an excuse for carrying on smoking endlessly just to find the 'right time', because there never is a right time. But if your motivation is so low at the moment that you know you aren't going to succeed, then it may be better for you to start the course afresh at a future date.

Some people think that taking a holiday helps, but the trouble is that on their return they are faced with all the old situations in which they used to smoke that the holiday took them away from. They think that they can have 'just one', and you know the cycle that follows.

One puff becomes one cigarette a day until one day it's one pack a day.

If there is a best time to do the course, then it's a time when you are under the normal pressures of life. That way you'll have a chance to understand why you smoke in those situations, which will be valuable information.

That's not to say that you should go and create havoc in your domestic lives in order to make the most out of the courses, though.

We talked about magic buttons in the very first chapter. There is the potential for total freedom from the enslaving smoking habit if you follow the course. To get to the magic button you first of all need to get through the assignments.

They aren't that difficult, really. All that you are being asked to do is to delay sticking a tube of vegetable matter into your mouth for short periods of time, and not to set fire to it. You absolutely can do this.

When I was trying to stop smoking using only my own willpower, the main factor that had me resume smoking after only a short period was that I was continually thinking about and wishing that I could smoke. I decided that I would rather die early than spend the rest of my life besotted with the fact that I couldn't smoke.

When I took the course, I could glimpse how the methods might work, but as with most smokers who have found staying off cigarettes uncomfortable in previous attempts, I was surprised just how easy not smoking was having prepared myself so thoroughly.

The most important difference was that although I still thought of cigarettes from time to time the thoughts never developed into cravings or longings.

And the number of times I thought about smoking diminished rapidly from Day One.

Occasionally I still felt a strong temptation to light up, but I knew that I had the mental 'tools' to ensure that I could survive until the thoughts of smoking had gone away.

Having succeeded you can see why the process worked.

But in the middle of doing the course all you have to go on are memories of previously unsuccessful attempts at giving up, coupled with your own perversity of actions and thoughts.

Stick with it for a couple of weeks more.

HOW DID YOU GET ON?

Start this week as usual by totalling your packstrap and transferring your daily and weekly totals onto your RECORD OF CIGARETTES on Page 33. Have your third packstrap handy and wrap it round your cigarette packet.

Are you smoking less yet? Don't worry if there hasn't been much change. Let's just review all of last week's assignments and see if there are any lessons that we have learnt.

Mark yourself out of ten for each of last week's assignments.

Oral gratification ....

Continue searching for taste ....

Continue observing smokers ....

Record each cigarette, plus alcohol and caffeine ....

Continue night-time recitation (Please try and remember this) ....

Change the dominant hand and side of mouth ....

Change brand to one you don't like ....

Change location of cigarettes ....

Get rid of your paraphernalia ....

Delay 30 minutes after meals ....

Delay ten minutes after tea and coffee ....

Delay ten minutes after alcohol ....

Total (out of a possible 120).

A few comments about these.

I found it interesting that when I remembered to change to smoking with my left hand, it felt uncomfortable and somehow affected my 'enjoyment' of the cigarette.

If you had any 'T's this week, go back to Session Two and reread the section on taste. Be sure that you are not confusing taste with 'satisfaction'.

I hope that you didn't find the alcohol assignment too difficult – it is very important to thoroughly break down these trigger situations before you get to 'Cut-off' point.

On with Session Three.

FATIGUE

When we talked about our reasons for smoking in an earlier session we saw that many people smoked when they were tired or felt that they needed a lift. We also saw that the same people also smoked when they wanted to relax.

Let's look at the actions of the drug nicotine a little more to see if we can explain some of this effect, and also see if we can make not smoking a bit easier with this knowledge.

Cigarette smoke introduces nicotine into your body's systems through the mouth tissues as well as via the lungs. Since nicotine is a powerful poison (you have probably heard that eight drops of nicotine injected into a horse will kill it), your body reacts.

Adrenalin and other hormones are released that bring your body temporarily into a state of increased alertness.

The same reaction would occur if you saw a dinosaur coming around the corner; your body would react to the threat by releasing sugar into the blood in order to give you the energy to run away or, if it was a small dinosaur, to hunt it for food. You may have heard of this 'flight or fight' mechanism before.

However, you don't take any vigorous physical exercise after each cigarette (and nor should you!) so the sugar content in your blood stays high, fooling your body's automatic monitoring system for maintaining correct and comfortable blood sugar levels.

You can think of it in very simple terms. Your monitoring system measures how much sugar there is in the blood, and if it has fallen below a certain level then it releases more from the liver.

If it reads the levels as high enough anyway, which it will do after a cigarette, then it won't release any. In fact, it will tend to overcompensate for the fact that suddenly you have very high blood sugar levels. Which means that when the cigarette's stimulus is over, you have less energy available to you than you would like.

So you have a cup of tea or coffee to give you another lift. That fools the body's automatic system even more, and after the burst from that cup of coffee has passed you need even more of a lift, and so you have the coffee and the cigarette together, this time for an even bigger lift.

At the end of the day, or earlier if you have poor eating habits, (people skipping breakfast or lunch, please note) you will end up feeling tired and generally fatigued.

You will be more susceptible to stress as you are placing

great strains on your body.

This isn't the place to go into a full discussion about stress and how to control it. There are many causes of stress, and there are many different ways of going about reducing the stresses in one's life.

However, there are two points that are important in understanding and coping with stress without cigarettes.

One is that you recognise that you use cigarettes as a distraction to problems, that they don't in any way help the eventual solution of the problem. It is not the cigarette that solves problems, it's you.

Secondly, you have got into a habit of using cigarettes automatically in stressful situations. Successful ex-smokers recognise early in their investigation that cigarettes actually create stressful conditions as heart rate increases, carbon monoxide is circulated through your blood rather than oxygen and the level of fat circulating in the bloodstream increases.

You have until now used smoking as a way of getting an immediate lift. Learn to do without that lift by keeping your energy levels more balanced throughout the day.

Most beneficial changes for people with high blood pressure problems, and for people with a high level of stress, come when sufferers can examine some of the behaviour patterns that lead to stress.

Anyone who finds themselves in a stressful lifestyle *can do something about it* simply by preparing themselves better.

Get sufficient rest and sufficient food for a start. Especially if you drive yourself hard all the time.

Change your eating habits if you can to allow more protein, more fresh food, and more fruit and vegetables.

Consider eating several light meals a day rather than a big meal late in the evening.

Start drinking orange juice when you want a lift rather than coffee or tea. Milk is good too, and can be calming to the nerves.

Do something about it rather than bemoan the fact that you've got a problem. Who else should be doing something about the fact that you're stressed?

Be good to yourself. Put yourself and your personal needs first for a change. Take at least half an hour during each day solely for you.

Learn to relax. Buy a relaxation tape or a book on relaxation. Or try stretching exercises and yoga.

Learn autogenics, or the Alexander technique.

Investigate some of the 'human potential' courses. Learn more about how your brain and body work.

Do the breathing exercise you learnt in the last session.

Take up regular exercise, as your health permits.

Lastly, plan your day to give yourself little rewards other than cigarettes through the day. Plan more excitement into your life.

I want to recap this subject of stress and fatigue. Smoking contributes to both stress and fatigue. Make progress toward a less stressful, and less fatigued life by looking after yourself more. Take a break. Give yourself a reward other than the usual tea, coffee or cigarette and then come back for the rest of the session.

Keep that perspective.

PEAK SMOKING PERIODS

Last week you worked out from your packstrap your Peak Smoking Periods and you made a note on your RECORD OF CIGARETTES. Now you should calculate your peak periods for this past week's smoking in the same way.

You'll have realised by now that you tend to smoke on cue. A cigarette goes hand in hand with a cup of coffee, and with your mother-in-law on the telephone, and at the end of a hard day's work.

Before I give too much of the game away, I would like you to examine the peak periods that your packstraps have shown over the past two weeks with a view to discovering exactly what was causing those peaks.

This is useful information.

The causes can be looked at in two ways, either situations in which a condition of discomfort is being relieved (like the aeroplane trip), or simply a habit situation (as at the end of each meal), or both.

I'll give you a helping hand.

I have classified four main peak periods through the day that are common to most people; the after breakfast period, mid-morning and mid-afternoon peaks, the early evening period, the mid to late evening period.

On the following page there are some examples of the reasons why these peaks occur. Look through your own peak periods and fill in your reasons in the spaces provided.

PEAK PERIODS DIAGRAM

You'll notice that fatigue is often a reason for a peak period. Make an extra special effort to look after your health over the next two or three weeks, and, as I have said, PAMPER YOURSELF.

ARE YOUR PEAK PERIODS THE SAME – OR DIFFERENT?

Time of Day	Possible Cause
Mid-Morning Slump	Fatigue and boredom – you need a lift, plenty of caffeine
Mid-Afternoon Slump	As above – after heavy lunches you feel tired
Pre-Dinner High Count	Cocktails before dinner, wine bars, relaxation time, kids coming home
Mid-Evening	Boredom, TV rut
After Breakfast	Stalling the day, need for nicotine
What are Your Peak Periods?	

Session Three

REPATTERNING

A young couple, recently married, had invited their relatives over for an evening meal.

As they were preparing the meal, the young man noticed his wife chopping off half an inch of the roast before putting it in the oven.

When he asked her why she performed this ritual, she replied, 'It's what my mother always used to do.'

Later in the evening, he asks his mother-in-law why she cuts an inch or so off the roast before cooking it. Her reply came: 'I don't know. It's what my mother always used to do.'

The young man can't sleep that night, beside himself with this question unanswered, and rushes off early in the morning to see his mother-in-law's mother to ask her the same question.

'Why do both your daughter, and your grand-daughter, slice a bit off their roasts?'

Her reply was obvious: 'I don't know why they do it, son. I had to cut pieces off to make the roast fit in my oven.'

All of us have patterns of behaviour which have become routine, and we are often totally unaware of the mechanical nature of many of our actions.

Some are patterns handed on to us from our parents, as in the example above. Some are routines that are simply tried and tested ways of getting things done. Some patterns of behaviour may have been important or necessary at an earlier time in our lives, but no longer serve their original purpose.

It is useful to observe your own behaviour and see just how rigid you are, often when there is no need to be.

Of course, there is much sense and logic behind most of our behaviour patterns, but you will find it interesting to notice your own patterns and wonder how they came to be there.

Smoking is one of those habits that no longer serves its original purpose. See what else comes under that category in your day-to-day life.

Do you react to emotional situations always in the same way? Do you always get defensive – or angry?

If you like, be imaginative this week. Look for different

things to do, and break loose a bit. Get yourself ready for a big celebration on your first day as a non-smoker in two weeks time, for a start.

ASSIGNMENTS Session Three

Watch out for the first signs of self-pity.

Assignment One
Switch to a brand in the low nicotine bracket, something with less than 0.9 mg nicotine.

Assignment Two
No night-time smoking. This is after you go to bed; no waking up in the middle of the night for a smoke.

Three tips. Thoroughly clean your mouth out before you go to bed, and if you wake up repeat the whole oral gratification procedure.

Also, a thermos of warm milk and honey kept by the bed may help with sleeplessness.

Put a no-smoking sign in your bedroom – make your bedroom a no-smoking area.

Assignment Three
No cigarettes before breakfast. Change your routines if necessary to achieve this satisfactorily. Remember that if one assignment is particularly difficult for you then you should concentrate especially hard in trying to be successful at that one – it will give you enormous confidence.

Assignment Four
Delay smoking 45 minutes AFTER ALL FOOD AND BEVERAGES excepting legal snacks.

Legal snacks are as follows:

water hot or cold
fruit or fruit juice
milk hot or cold
raw vegetables
consommé or bouillon.

You'll note that alcohol, tea or coffee are *not* on the list.

Succeed with this assignment and you've got it licked.

Most people experience the odd moments of difficulty. But there are ways around most seemingly difficult situations.

For instance, if you want a drink at the pub, or at a party, then plan your evening well.

Smoke a couple of cigarettes so that you boost your nicotine level and then have a drink. After you've finished the drink you've got 45 minutes to go before you can have your next cigarette. Drink water, or fruit juice if you like, or get up and walk around a bit.

After the 45 minutes are up, light up. Smoke two cigarettes in quick succession if you like, and then order another drink and start the process again.

(You don't have to wait 45 minutes after the cigarette for the drink.)

With tea and coffee it's somewhat easier.

Normally we drink coffee and smoke as well. Now you can have the cigarette first, followed by the coffee, but not the other way round.

If you are working in a group do get support from your fellow participants. If you can crack this assignment, you'll have little difficulty further on.

Assignment Five
No cigarette 45 minutes before bedtime. A good time to relax, go over your reasons for stopping, add to your list of assets and so on.

Assignment Six
No cigarette while writing or typing. Again, this one is not as difficult as it sounds.

You'll probably notice that when you are actually writing or typing, the cigarette is in the ashtray. It's only when you come up for air that the cigarette gets into your lips.

All you need do to succeed at this assignment is to stop writing or typing while you smoke the cigarette. Put it out and then go back to what you were doing.

Assignment Seven
Try not to dwell on the delay times.

Assignment Eight
Get enough sleep to help avoid fatigue.

Assignment Nine
Eat three well-balanced meals a day for the same reason.

Assignment Ten
Add (or start) 5 minutes exercise per day to your existing regime.

Assignment Eleven
Start rewarding yourself in ways other than cigarettes.

Assignment Twelve
Begin developing contempt for cigarettes.

Assignment Thirteen
Continue drinking 4 glasses of water per day.

Assignment Fourteen
Arrange a chest X-ray. Call your local doctor or surgery to arrange this – in some places there are mobile units, otherwise you can normally arrange a free check up.

This isn't obligatory, this assignment, but having the X-ray can remove any worries that you might have.

Some CLOSING THOUGHTS this week.

- You are now aware of each cigarette.
- You are developing a distaste and genuine contempt for smoking.
- You are happy to have a clean mouth feeling.
- You are beginning to believe that you can live happily without cigarettes.
- You will stop smoking, you will feel better, you will be free.

4

4

SESSION FOUR

PUTTING IT ALL TOGETHER

Hello again. This is my favourite session to teach.

Bring yourself up to date by transferring the daily and weekly total of the cigarettes you've smoked onto the RECORD OF CIGARETTES form back on Page 33.

Many of the concepts that we have been discussing are brought together for the final week before you put your cigarettes down for good.

HAVING TROUBLE WITH THE ASSIGNMENTS?

As usual, we'll start by looking through last week's assignments, and unlike the discussion in the previous three sessions when I have harped on about the necessity of doing the assignments, this time I'm going to start the session by forgiving a few mistakes.

Obviously, if you have got this far then you must be at least fairly committed to stopping this time and succeeding.

And if you are one of the many people who have tried giving up before, but have reverted to smoking for one reason or another, then I do want to reassure you that you haven't completely ruined your chances of succeeding if you found it difficult to complete the assignments 100 per cent during this last week.

Almost everyone who joins our courses falls short during this third week, either with the three-quarters of an hour delay time after alcohol, or after food or both.

Some people have more difficulty with the early morning delay, the delay before breakfast.

I have seen people succeed on the course who smoked more than 180 cigarettes during the week that they were due to stop. I have seen people succeed and almost completely ignore the assignments during the third week.

It's not advisable, but as I have said before, it is *your decision* to stop smoking that will ensure your success beyond all other factors.

The assignments serve an extremely useful purpose. They help to break down the 'trigger situations' that send you reaching for a cigarette on cue. Following the assignments well means that you'll tend to think of smoking much less frequently when you've stopped because you will have already reprogrammed yourself not to smoke in most of your normal smoking situations.

Performing the assignments also helps concentrate your mind on your objective of learning how not to want to smoke by helping you gain an understanding into the mechanisms that make up your own smoking behaviour.

If you successfully complete the assignments, then you will be feeling good about yourself – having had some successes will leave your confidence high.

It is rare that anyone in the seminars completes this last week's projects perfectly. The most common problem assignment is the delay after alcohol. It's all to easy to lose touch with your determination to 'follow the rules' at parties and similar social occasions.

Many smokers can't imagine living an active social life without cigarettes, especially as a drink and a cigarette seem to go hand in hand.

Certainly, I found it almost unthinkable that I could spend the rest of my life at parties desperately trying not to think of cigarettes.

If the social occasions are the ones that you are most worried about, it is important to build up your own confidence by succeeding at the assignments concerning alcohol most of the time during this run up to Cut-Off Day.

There is no point in simply avoiding booze, (or tea or coffee for that matter) because when you next have a drink (or tea or coffee) after you have stopped smoking you will find that you will be reminded of a cigarette because you haven't yet broken that association.

IT IS EXTREMELY IMPORTANT TO BREAK THIS ASSOCIATION BEFORE CUT-OFF DAY.

So please, make an extra-special effort this week. After all, it's only for one week more.

ARE YOU AT ALL WORRIED THAT YOU WON'T SUCCEED?

We've talked a lot about self-worth, and the effects that differing attitudes can have on one's ability to succeed at anything in life. But never mind how much we try to focus our attention on the positive aspects of problems, we all carry around with us our own doubts about our ability, the unconfident side of our nature.

We have found it useful to examine some of our fears, not necessarily to analyse them and try and explain them, but because simply acknowledging fears does seem to alleviate the burden of worrying about them.

What I'd like to ask you to do is as follows:

Write on the following two pages all your fears, hesitations and worries about 'giving up' smoking.

Complete the sentence:

'I don't think I'm going to be able to succeed on this course and stop smoking because:

....'

I'll help you with a couple of examples, but there won't be a list that you can check against. It's up to you to make the most of this exercise.

You don't necessarily have to believe that you will give in to any of your areas of concern, but do try and see what is going on in the back of your mind. These are some examples:

'I don't think that I will be able to succeed because I have been hopeless with the assignments.'

Or because:

– I simply can't believe it can be possible to stop smoking easily
– I can't imagine or see myself as a non-smoker
– I'm still not convinced I don't enjoy it

Get the idea?

Give yourself ten minutes for this exercise. You should try to list about fifteen items, not as a drudge, but as a chance to see what you're up against.

To repeat, Werner Erhard, talking about getting what you want from life, said that you can either have what you want in this life, or you can have your reasons for not having it.

Some of the fears you are expressing in this exercise are remarkably similar to excuses that you might make if you choose to start smoking again.

Everyone is capable of stopping smoking. You do it every time you put out a cigarette. It's not lighting up the next one that is the problem. If you can see the tricks that your own mind plays on you to rationalise starting smoking again you can be better prepared simply by facing up to it.

Carry on with the exercise.

If you find yourself stuck, unable to think of more fears, sit back and close your eyes for a minute. Take a couple of deep breaths, close your eyes and relax. When you're comfortable say to yourself out loud,

'I don't think that I will be able to succeed at stopping smoking because . . . . .' and then see what comes into your mind.

Take your time over this.

I DON'T THINK THAT I WILL BE ABLE TO SUCCEED AT STOPPING SMOKING ON THIS COURSE BECAUSE. . . .

Done enough? Get up and stretch yourself.

Then do the last exercise one more time. Ask yourself if there isn't any worry that you do know you have, but you're not sure you want to admit it to yourself. Put that one down.

Onward . . . .

For this next exercise I would like you to sit back in your chair and relax. Unfold your arms and legs and close your eyes when you've got the general idea.

Imagine that it's a warm summery evening sometime in the future. Imagine yourself sitting outside in a quiet garden or park, sitting on a bench or a deck-chair, or behind a tree or anywhere you feel comfortable.

It's one of your favourite spots.

You can smell the flowers, and the freshly cut hay, and you can hear the noises of summer, the birds in the trees and crickets in the hedges. You can feel the warm gentle wind on your forehead, and you are sitting relaxed, content and at peace with yourself.

Sit there for a couple of moments simply taking in the environment.

Concentrate on your breathing. Breathe in and then breathe slowly and steadily out. And, while you're breathing regularly, remind yourself of the garden that you're in.

After a couple of minutes, I want you to imagine a close friend joining you in your scene. When he or she sits down beside you, I want you to picture both of you chatting to one another.

Imagine you're having a conversation about your experience of succeeding at stopping smoking.

About how proud you feel of yourself.

Of how much better you feel in every way – you can smell the flowers better, you can run upstairs without getting out of breath.

Imagine what *you* would say to your friend.

When you have said all that you want to say, open your eyes and write down what it felt like to be a non-smoker.

Start imagining.

Write down some of the things that you told your friend.

MAIN THEME OF THE COURSE

And now we're back to the central theme of the course – that you smoke on cue to various signals from your environment. Some of these signals are internal and some are external.

From last week's session you'll remember that internal signals might be hunger, or feeling tired, and they also include emotional states such as being depressed or ecstatic, frustated or angry.

External signals range from your best friend offering you a cigarette, to associations that you've built up over the years as with the cigarette and the drink, or the cup of tea.

Here's a checklist Add your own ones to the list:

Internal Signals	**External Signals**
Boredom	Someone else lights up
Frustration	Advertisement catches your eye
Anger	Telephone rings
Upset	Cup of coffee
Loneliness	End of meal
Tiredness	Seeing friends
Feeling ecstatic	

Why are you smoking this cigarette?

Time	a x C O	Day

MY PEAK PERIOD TODAY WAS BETWEEN________AND________

Why are you smoking this cigarette?

Time	a x C O	Day

NEW PACKSTRAP

This week your packstrap is of a different design. This week you'll be recording not only the time that you lit up, but also the reason why you want to smoke at that particular time. You will need one of these packstraps for each day of this week, so you must photocopy the one opposite seven times.

The whole emphasis of this week's assignments is to get you to focus on each and every cigarette that you smoke and to understand why you are lighting it.

You are asked to fill in the reason why you have lit each cigarette – at the time of lighting.

Sometimes the reasons will be obvious, sometimes you might find it difficult to find a reason.

If you can't easily find a reason, that should be useful information in itself.

It might help to try asking yourself just before you light up:

IF I DON'T WANT TO BE A SMOKER ANYMORE, BUT I THINK I WANT A CIGARETTE – WHAT IS IT THAT I REALLY WANT?

TAKE NOTE OF THAT SENTENCE. IT'S A KEY IDEA

Also make a note of the time that you smoke each cigarette, but you can forget the recording of alcohol and caffeine from now on. (Though the delay times still apply.)

REWARDS

Cigarettes are often used as rewards.

Just as you would give a horse a lump of sugar after a well-executed jump, so people will allow themselves a cigarette as a reward after they have finished a particular piece of work, be it the quarterly VAT return or the ironing.

It is so easy to reward oneself with a cigarette that smokers don't often try very hard to find other rewards.

If you use cigarettes as a reward, it will feel like something is missing from your life when you've stopped smoking, unless you have other things to look forward to.

Believe it or not, you may even feel that 'life is pointless' unless you are able to light up and get your customary dose of nicotine.

Human beings are strange. I have been told of experiments done in prisons where the prisoners' privileges were steadily removed to examine the threshold at which the prisoners would riot.

Taking their cigarettes away from them produced more reaction than anything else.

Think about it for a moment.

Are cigarettes the basis of your existence? If you weren't to smoke ever again, would that really remove your purpose and direction in life?

Of course not!

But it may feel as though something is missing from your life for a while after you've put out your last cigarette.

To help you through this period it may be useful to plan some additional excitement into your life.

I've given you a list of one hundred rewards or activities you might enjoy.

Choose at least one different reward each day for the next week. Make sure you take time out for yourself this week. Do something specifically for *you* every day.

You matter.

LIST OF REWARDS

Here's a four-month supply of rewards and distractions that are neither costly nor fattening. Try one each day – treats, adventures, activities designed to put some added zest into your life.

For the next three weeks, sample a new one each day for a total of 21 days. Out of these, select the seven best and write them on the last page of this list so that they become seven rewards that you would like to permanently integrate into your lifestyle

☐ 1 Buy yourself some flowers.
☐ 2 Have breakfast in bed.
☐ 3 Pack yourself a picnic and eat it in the park during your lunch hour.
☐ 4 Fly a kite, play a game of 'frisbee.'
☐ 5 Try a new cologne, perfume, aftershave.
☐ 6 Make time to listen to your favourite records.
☐ 7 Take up a new hobby.
☐ 8 Join a choir, take singing lessons.
☐ 9 Invent a salad recipe.
☐10 Send someone you've been taking for granted a love letter.
☐11 Analyse your handwriting.
☐12 Write a letter to your MP.
☐13 Call on someone elderly who would really appreciate your visit.
☐14 Do someone an unsolicited favour, just because you feel like it, or because you want to create a surprise effect.
☐15 Read a new magazine.
☐16 Make a phone call to an old friend, or call a recent acquaintance to cultivate a new friendship.
☐17 Take a twenty minute nap.
☐18 Carry a book with you all the time and flip it open when you're kept waiting, are bored, or have an extra two minutes.
☐19 Reward yourself often with thoughts about freedom from smoking.
☐20 Clean your car inside and out; enjoy a clean vehicle. Some baking soda in the ashtrays will eliminate that stale smell.

☐21 Go horseriding.
☐22 Resume a favourite, long-neglected hobby.
☐23 Drive into the country and smell the clean, fresh air.
☐24 Get a new hair style . . . cut it short, or change the colour.
☐25 Take a mini-holiday or long weekend.
☐26 Wear something special that you've been saving.
☐27 Treat yourself to a long distance phone call to a far-away friend or relative.
☐28 Go for a bike ride, and feel the breeze blow through your hair.
☐29 Rent a bicycle if you don't have one; try getting to work that way.
☐30 Have a massage.
☐31 Visit your local library. Join it and use it.
☐32 Adopt a tree on your street and plant some flowers or ivy in its bed.
☐33 Go roller skating.
☐34 Rent a rowing boat for an hour.
☐35 Make yourself a hammock and take a nap in it; hang it indoors for winter.
☐36 Watch birds . . . build a birdhouse outside your window.
☐37 Read your horoscope.
☐38 Buy some exotic fresh fruits along with the more familiar ones, and make yourself a different fruit salad.
☐39 Go fishing off a public pier.
☐40 Buy new running shoes.
☐41 Have a manicure; a pedicure.
☐42 Visit the zoo, or a museum, or a local tourist attraction in your lunch hour. Or any time.
☐43 Buy a bestseller in hardcover instead of waiting for the paperback edition to come out.
☐44 Update your photo album, or edit your slide collection.
☐45 Try a new recipe, or invent a new one with your food processor.
☐46 Buy a raffle ticket or do the pools.
☐47 Plant a window-sill herb garden.
☐48 Adopt a pet from the RSPCA.
☐49 Find some music on the radio and dance to it.
☐50 Read and record for the blind.
☐51 Have dinner by candlelight.
☐52 Go for a swim.

☐53 Be a kid again! Plan something to look forward to the way a child does.
☐54 Take some time just for yourself.
☐55 Take a bubble bath, or a bracing shower.
☐56 Treat yourself to lessons: bridge, dance, tennis, swimming, cooking, a foreign language.
☐57 Browse in an antique shop, sporting goods shop, hardware shop, card shop, craft shop, book shop. . .
☐58 Sleep late.
☐59 Have your teeth cleaned and admire them.
☐60 Have a chest X-ray.
☐61 Throw out your ugly ashtrays and turn your nice ones into plant pots.
☐62 Buy yourself some coloured felt-tip pens for writing notes.
☐63 Buy a goldfish and care for it.
☐64 Take up a musical instrument – guitar, recorder, piano, drums. . .
☐65 Attend a series of lectures – at the museum, library, church, adult education centre.
☐66 Buy yourself a kit – any kind – and put something together: a boat, bookshelves, radio set, craft projector. . .
☐67 Use the car ashtray for loose change and parking receipts.
☐68 Go for a walk through a gentle rain shower or a field of flowers.
☐69 Go for a walk through crunchy autumn leaves.
☐70 Go for a romp through the snow . . . have a snowball fight with a friend.
☐71 Write a letter to an editor.
☐72 Build a window box and plant something in it. Paint it a cheerful colour; embellish it with some design.
☐73 Jog before breakfast.
☐74 Begin to plan something really fun and different for your holiday this year – make it a real adventure.
☐75 Create mental image rewards – 'day-dream-pictures,' pleasant memories, thoughts about wonderful future events, fantasies (sexual, creative, adventurous) – whatever kind you like.
☐76 Watch a spectacular sunrise or a breathtaking sunset.
☐77 Raise a sunflower – the biggest in captivity.

☐78 Take your pulse now that you've stopped smoking.
☐79 Find a secret place to go skinny-dipping.
☐80 Go for a walk in the woods, or by the shore, and bring your sketchpad.
☐81 Leave a message for yourself on your telephone answering machine, or on your tape recorder, or by dropping a letter in the mail, to congratulate yourself on how great you are now that you don't smoke anymore.
☐82 Watch a movie.
☐83 Solve a crossword puzzle.
☐84 Make a list of good eating places.
☐85 Look up what happened in the newspaper the day you were born.
☐86 Listen to birdcalls, and try to identify them.
☐87 Design your dream house.
☐88 Play Monopoly.
☐89 Learn to read faster.
☐90 Take a walk in the woods to look for wild flowers.
☐91 Research your family history.
☐92 Sleep out under the stars.
☐93 Volunteer at party headquarters for the political candidate of your choice.
☐94 Sample the first apples and first cider of the season.
☐95 Go back to bed after sending the kids to school.
☐96 Read your 'Assets List' and feel cheered.
☐97 Plan an exciting evening at home with the family (without the television set!)
☐98 Treat yourself to a first class train ticket.
☐99 Dry some autumn flowers and arrange them in an old wine bottle.
☐100 Knit yourself a sweater.
☐101 Visit a long-lost relative.
☐102 Start writing that book you've been promising you'd write someday.
☐103 Create your own list of ways to reward yourself with things that are neither costly nor fattening!
☐104
☐105
☐106
☐107
☐108
☐109

The famous canine philosopher, Snoopy, once said: 'Anticipation is the greater part of joy.' Plan your rewards.

The successful seven rewards I would most like to incorporate into my lifestyle are as follows

1____________________________________

2____________________________________

3____________________________________

4____________________________________

5____________________________________

6____________________________________

7____________________________________

SYMPTOMS OF RECOVERY

Don't you think that's a better word than withdrawal symptoms?

While the nicotine is being removed from your system your body will take a little while to adjust.

After all, this may well be the first time that your adult body has known a drug-free life.

Depending on individual differences in smoking patterns, length of time one has smoked, and individual differences in body make-up, different people experience different 'symptoms of recovery'.

These include feeling irritable, feeling tired and restless, stomach upsets, thirst, muddle-headedness and some other unpleasant side-effects.

You may even find that you get drunker quicker as your alcohol tolerance may decrease.

All of these side-effects are transient – that is to say they won't last for long, usually a matter of weeks.

If you do notice any of the following symptoms, blame them on nicotine withdrawal and welcome the signs that mean that the drug is leaving your body.

Normally all the symptoms will have left by the seventh session, two weeks after you've finally stopped. Do, of course, visit a doctor if any of the symptoms persist or are unusually uncomfortable.

I've listed here thirty common symptoms of recovery.

As different people react differently, you may not have noticed any change at all – yet. Nevertheless, take a look at the list and be forewarned – very few people seem to suffer no symptoms.

Tick any of the following symptoms of recovery you may have experienced.

Bleeding gums	Constipation	Tingly fingers
Sore tongue	Itchiness	Headache
Muddleheadedness	Diarrhoea	Dizziness
Insomnia	Sinus congestion	Stiffness
Flatulence	Nervousness	Vision changes
Fluid retention	Swelling	Heightened awareness
Acid indigestion/ heartburn	Depression	Lethargy
	Leg pains	Nausea
Sleepiness	Shooting pains	Lack of concentration
Irritability	Skin eruption	Low alcohol threshold
Thirst	Coughing	

WHO IS YOUR BEST FRIEND?

Sit back for a moment and relax.

I want you to imagine this. Your best friend calls you from hospital telling you that she (or he) has been taken ill and needs your help. Obviously you want to do anything you can for her.

The most important thing seems to be taking her mind off all her normal chores and day-to-day worries, so that she can concentrate on getting herself better.

Would you look after your best friend in need?

Start thinking of yourself as your own best friend and for the remainder of the course think of yourself as ill, but on the road to recovery.

Give yourself the following prescriptions:

1 Give yourself a break – don't get yourself involved in things that aren't important to you. Leave the trivia behind.

2 Pamper yourself. You would gladly have taken your friend grapes, flowers and anything that could aid her recovery. Do the same for yourself this week; treat yourself – a new haircut, visit a friend, do any of the 100 rewards on the list.

3 Look after yourself. Get sufficient sleep. Eat well.

4 Develop a more calm and serene attitude. All situations can be handled more easily when you are calm, and people will respect you more. Count to ten before getting involved in a problem. Remember your breathing exercise. Try and put any matter that's upsetting you into perspective – will it be important in ten years' time?

MIRROR TALK

I want you to start a 'Mirror Talk' exercise.

It may feel a little uncomfortable at first talking to yourself in the mirror, but our research has indicated that this exercise is extremely valuable.

For two minutes each day you should look at yourself in the

mirror and simply say out loud (or to yourself if someone's listening):

I WILL STOP SMOKING,
I WILL FEEL BETTER,
I WILL LOOK BETTER,
I WILL BE FREE.

Before long you will find yourself believing it.

Try the exercise once before you continue with the rest of the session.

Before we go on to the assignments for this week, I want to review some of the information that we've covered since the first session.

At the first session we started looking at why you started smoking, why you carry on smoking and your attitudes towards stopping and 'giving up'.

Since that first session you have been discovering the real reasons why you smoke.

You have noticed that you do seem to smoke on cue in various different situations and we have been breaking up those 'trigger' associations.

Although breaking up the physical aspects of the habit is crucial, your mental attitude is still the main determinant of whether you are going to be successful or not.

One key idea that I have been trying to get over is that cigarettes ***aren't as enjoyable as you thought they were.***

As the assignments have continued you have probably noticed that your concept of enjoyment has changed as you have had to change little bits about your habit and you have spent time thinking about smoking.

I found this most striking when I had to change the normal hand that I held my cigarette in. Suddenly smoking wasn't so enjoyable. Why should I get any less 'enjoyment' out of smoking with my left hand than with my right?

So we're coming to the conclusion that the 'enjoyment' is in the habit, not in the cigarette itself.

Remember, if you will, your first ever cigarette. That one wasn't enjoyable, was it?

This week's assignments will illustrate this point about enjoyment even more clearly than hitherto. I hope what you find out will finally persuade you that the 'enjoyment' of smoking is to a large extent an illusion.

Remember the 'discomfort theory'?

Simply put you are being asked to concentrate only on your cigarette when you are smoking during this last week.

In other words, when you have a cigarette this week make sure that you are doing nothing else at the same time, no working, watching TV and so on.

Nothing that will distract you from the cigarette.

You are asked, this week, along with writing down the reason that you are smoking, to do nothing else apart from smoke when you are smoking.

ASSIGNMENTS Session Four

Spot the self-pity.

Assignment One
Read through your original list of Assets and Dreams and try and add a further ten in each category.

Assignment Two
Do the same with your Reasons for Stopping Smoking.

Assignment Three
Change to the lowest nicotine brand you can find.

Assignment Four
Record everything on your new packstrap – the time that you lit up and the reason for it.

Assignment Five
Increase all delay times to one hour. That's one hour delay after each meal, after all food and beverages, before going to bed and after awakening. Try your hardest to succeed 100 per cent.

Assignment Six
Do not stop smoking before your scheduled Cut-Off Day even if you are finding continuing to smoke with all the restrictions rather frustrating.

Assignment Seven
No smoking while on the telephone. You will probably find this surprisingly simple, even if you are a telephonist. Just don't do it!

Assignment Eight
No smoking in the car or on any public transport.

Assignment Nine
No smoking while typing, writing, knitting, sewing, watching TV or reading.

Assignment Ten
In fact the only time that you are allowed to smoke is when you are doing nothing except smoking.

Give each cigarette all your attention, and mark your reason on your new packstrap.

Assignment Eleven
Do not sit in your favourite armchair watching TV or reading the newspaper.

Assignment Twelve
Go on a cigarette hunt. Make sure you have none around your home to tempt you after next week. Keep only the one pack of cigarettes you are using.

Assignment Thirteen
Collect your cigarette butts this week, and bring them with you to the next session in a jam jar.

Assignment Fourteen
Re-read your reasons for stopping smoking every day, and re-read your entire notebook this week.

Assignment Fifteen
Practise mirror talk twice daily. That's telling yourself that you are going to stop smoking out loud in front of a mirror.

Assignment Sixteen
Look after yourself, get sufficient rest, relaxation and good food.

Assignment Seventeen
Reward yourself often and take plenty of time purely for yourself.

The assignments are difficult this week, I know. But you are now only a week away from one of the most important gifts that you can give yourself in a lifetime – the gift of freedom from a dangerous, addictive and unpleasant habit.

Do your best.

REMEMBER YOU CAN EITHER HAVE WHAT YOU WANT OR YOUR REASONS FOR NOT HAVING IT.

Here are some suggestions you might like to consider:

- You are beginning to see the possibility of being free.
- You are eager and less afraid – in fact quite anxious to be done with it.

- Your body is already responding to the reduction of nicotine.
- Your mind is responding to increased self-worth and confidence.
- You are aware that stopping smoking is one of the most important things in your life.

So strengthen your resolve to be free. Do all that you can to complete the assignments this week. Smoke as though your life depended upon it.

The potential for complete freedom from this enslaving habit is here – it depends upon you.

Have you missed out or skipped over anything?

Work at it.

It's worth it.

Have a good week.

5

5

SESSION FIVE

TAKE A DEEP BREATH

Well, this is the bit you've been waiting for.

This session will bring together all the information we've discussed over the past weeks so that you will *know* that ***you are ready to stop***.

I'll be telling you how you'll deal with your last ever cigarette and I'll be giving you plenty of hints and suggestions as to how to make the coming weeks as easy as possible.

Nervous? Most people are to some extent.

You don't need to be though. If you have followed the assignments and understood the concepts, then you are as prepared to quit smoking as you will ever be.

You may feel a little apprehensive. That's normal, particularly if you tried to stop before but started again later.

But don't worry. You have spent four weeks getting ready for tomorrow. You are ready.

Remember the three parts to the COMPULSIVE SMOKING SYNDROME that we talked about in the first session – the physical addiction to nicotine, the psychological aspects of smoking including the automatic and the emotional cigarettes and also the social aspects of smoking.

THE PHYSICAL ADDICTION

The amount of nicotine in your system should be about 20 per cent of what it was some four weeks ago.

Turn to Page 33 and fill in the RECORD OF CIGARETTES for the past week's cigarettes.

Now, work out how much your intake has dropped since you started the course. The figures in brackets are my examples; fill in your own in the spaces provided.

How many cigarettes did you estimate that you smoked in an average week? (Before you started the course)
——— (140)

How much nicotine was there in the brand?
——— (1.4 mg)

So you started with (140 x 1.4 = 196 mg of nicotine per week)

—————

How many cigarettes did you smoke last week?
——— (60)

How much nicotine in last week's brand? ——— (0.5 mg)

So you now have about (30 mg) in your system ———

A reduction from 196 mg to 30 mg is a reduction of about 85 per cent of the original nicotine!

Put in your own figures and calculate how much you have reduced your intake.

If you don't get on with maths – ask someone else to work it out for you. It's worth knowing!

***How* Much? *That* Much?**

No wonder you've been having symptoms of recovery!

Almost all of the remaining nicotine in your system will be gone within 72 hours. After that period any cravings that you'll be having are more likely to be due to the habit, *not* the effect of the drug. This means you have control over the outcome.

So we've dealt with the physical addiction.

PSYCHOLOGICAL FACTORS

I would be surprised if you had lit many cigarettes without being aware of them during this last week.

Unless, that is, you forgot that alcohol can have a stronger effect when you're stopping smoking.

You've broken up most of your conditioned responses, the trigger mechanisms that used to send you reaching for a cigarette. The 'automatic' cigarettes are pretty much gone.

Because of this, you may well be surprised tomorrow to find that you aren't thinking about cigarettes nearly as much as you thought you would. Even if you do think about them the 'craving' will not be there.

Keep your eyes and ears open for the danger times – times when you're smoking for an emotional reason, for example, and just remember:

Cigarettes are one problem you don't need.

In particular, be on your guard when you are feeling sorry for yourself – it's all too easy to give in when you are feeling down.

You know that *cigarettes don't make anything any better*. If you do light up you'll only feel worse about yourself, whereas not giving in to your desire to smoke in such circumstances may be the boost to your ego that you need to start making yourself feel better.

Smoking will never make you feel better.

SOCIAL FACTORS

While you may find that not smoking is difficult in certain social situations you know that social pressure is as a whole favouring the non-smoker.

Insurance premiums are higher, non-smokers are beginning to complain about sidestream smoke. Smoking does seem to have lost much of its 'romantic appeal'.

Try not to be too hard on others who still smoke when you have stopped, though. You know how it feels to have some righteous do-gooder preaching at you about the evils of smoking.

If someone offers you a cigarette, just let them know that you don't smoke. And leave it at that.

So, believe it or not, you are prepared.

It may not feel like it, but you are.

Are you concerned that you haven't done the assignments sufficiently well to make the process easy? Then let me give you some good news.

If you were aiming an arrow at a target some distance away you would aim the bow into the air, knowing that the arrow would fall back down under the force of gravity as it neared the target.

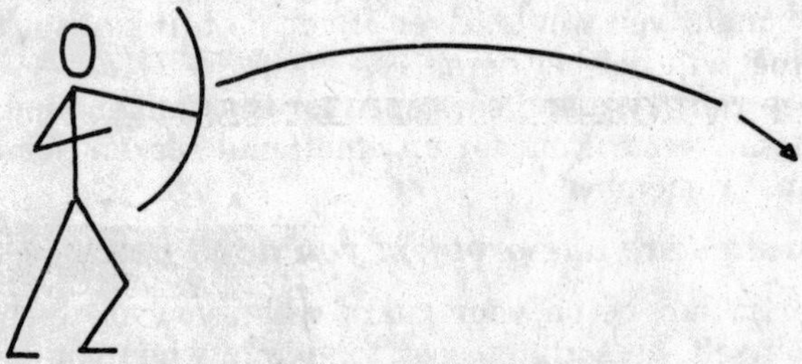

I went on and on in the first two sessions about the necessity of completing the assignments 100 per cent.

In fact, you were expected to fall short occasionally. I set the targets higher than necessary so that you would succeed comfortably.

Seventy per cent of the assignments completed satisfactorily should ensure that you find the withdrawal experience fairly painless. I have seen people succeed even though they have completely ignored the entire fourth week's assignments.

It's not recommended, though.

Of course, if you have continually cheated on one particular assignment (for example if you have never waited the full delay time after a drink), then you may find that there are some situations in which not smoking is still going to be uncomfortable.

Even so, you'll be given a list of tips to help in those situations later this session.

So don't worry! Although you may be apprehensive about what tomorrow will bring, you are as prepared for stopping smoking as you will ever be.

**REMEMBER
NO ONE EVER DIED
FROM
STOPPING SMOKING!**

For the remainder of today, the rules are relaxed. You may smoke as much as you like, when you like – with one stipulation that you don't increase the strength of the cigarettes.

When I took the course, I smoked only 57 cigarettes during the whole of the last week. Then I smoked twelve cigarettes between finishing that session and going to bed about three hours later.

My mother had about 40 the night before she stopped.

THAT'S PROBABLY A BIT EXCESSIVE.

So let the reins drop and enjoy yourself tonight, without being silly about it.

It is the last night you will ever smoke, after all!

Last Week's Assignments

Let's quickly review the assignments for last week to see if there was anything to learn from them.

Once again, mark yourself out of 10 for how well you completed them.

1	Change to lowest brand	....
2	Record everything on new pack-strap	....
3	Delay smoking one hour after all food and beverages	....
	and after waking and before retiring	....
4	Do not 'Cut-Off' early	....
5	No smoking on the telephone	....
6	No smoking in the car or on transport	....
7	No smoking while typing, reading, writing, watching TV, knitting or sewing	....
8	Smoke only when you are smoking (i.e. when doing nothing else)	....

9	Do not smoke in your favourite armchair	....
10	Go on a cigarette hunt	....
11	Collect your cigarette butts	....
12	Re-read your notebook	....
13	Practise mirror talk	....
14	Look after yourself, eat and sleep well	....
15	Do one different reward from the list each day	....
16	Keep your butts	....

There were two main points I wanted you to notice about your smoking this week.

Firstly, having to write down a reason as to why you were smoking each cigarette should have been instructive. Many people find that their real reason for smoking is considerably different from the one they expected.

I know someone who 'knew' that she smoked mainly when under stress. She was an extremely intelligent woman who was perhaps more aware than most of her own behaviour. During the week in which she had to write down her reasons for smoking, she found to her surprise that it wasn't stress after all – that in fact she smoked as a reward rather than anything else.

Most people find the exercise of smoking on their own, doing nothing else apart from smoking, highly informative.

Often, although the first couple of puffs seem to be important, they discover that really there is nothing much to smoking apart from 'injecting' themselves with a small dose of nicotine, sticking a tube of vegetables into your mouth, setting fire to it and breathing in poisonous chemicals.

In fact, most people find it extremely frustrating simply smoking and doing nothing else besides.

What does this tell you? Well, you should know by now exactly what you mean by 'enjoyment' and how much of it you'll really be 'giving up':

Is it really that much?

So you are as prepared *as you are ever going to be.*

Tonight you are going to smoke your **last cigarette**.

Make sure you have enough cigarettes to last you until you go to bed.

Tomorrow has the potential for being one of the most exciting and satisfying days of your life. I make sure I celebrate the anniversary of the day I stopped smoking every year.

Make smoking and disposing of that last cigarette tonight a ritual. Set aside time so that you can be alone for your final smoke.

Get yourself into the right frame of mind for the last cigarette by re-reading your notebook, especially looking at your reasons for succeeding.

Run your eyes over any sections of this book that you've found particularly valuable.

As you smoke this last cigarette, tell yourself how pleased you are that you will no longer have to be a slave to smoking – a slave to guilt, dirty ashtrays, nicotine-stained fingers and so on.

Ceremoniously dispose of your last cigarette down the loo.

FAREWELL, CRUEL WORLD!

By the way, if the cigarette comes back after the flush – it's NOT an Act of God!

This is no time for a change of heart. No 'Farewell Old Friend You are getting rid of one of your worst enemies, not an ol friend.

From tomorrow on you will not want to smoke. Thought of smoking may occur but the compulsion to smoke will b gone.

You will be delighted that you no longer smoke.

THIS IS IT
THIS IS YOUR LAST CIGARETTE

Do not be afraid.

Blame everything bad next week on stopping smoking, you physical distress and your state of mind. Ask your friends an colleagues to support you through the first couple of week without cigarettes.

Attribute any benefits to stopping smoking as well.

Look out for any improvements to your health, to your pock or comments from friends about how well you're doin

Reinforce your new habit of not smoking by looking out for positive signs.

If you are having a few moments of difficulty then remember **CVS to BVS** – concentrate on the positive.

Avoid feeling sorry for yourself if you can help it. Otherwise try and adopt a 'Well, if I can get through this, I can get through anything' attitude.

If you can get through one tricky situation, you can get through another.

THE LIFETIME COST OF SMOKING

It will help you maintain your resolve if you find out what your next cigarette might cost you.

We're going to do an exercise to calculate how much money you have already spent on cigarettes, and how much you would be spending in the future if you don't stop now.

How much have you spent on smoking so far?

1 Average smoked per day at Meeting No. 1:

[ ] ×365 = [ ] average smoked yearly.

2 Total average smoked yearly:

[ ] × number of years smoked = [ ] total smoked to date.

3 Total smoked to date:

[ ] ÷ 20 (i.e. 1 pack) = no. of packs smoked to date.

= [ ] × average past cost per pack (assume £1.55)

4 TOTAL COST TO DATE. £ [ ]

How much you could spend in the future.

1 Actual number of cigarettes smoked per day (at time you joined *HabitBreakers*):

[ ] × 365 = [ ] total smoked yearly.

2 Total smoked yearly:

[ ] × 80 years minus your age (i.e. if you're 30 multiply by 50) = [ ]

3 Total you could have smoked (if you live to be 80):

[ ] ÷ 20 = no. of packs

[ ] × average cost per pack (£1.55) = [ ]

4 Projected Cost between now and when you're 80 **IF YOU DID NOT STOP**: [ ]

5 Then add Total Cost To Date: to find

YOUR LIFETIME COST OF SMOKING £

Return on investment.

Divide projected cost between now and when you're 80 by the cost of this book:

This is the number of times your investment will be returned now that you've stopped.

A not inconsiderable sum.

I worked out that if I were to start smoking again it would cost me about £42,000. A fairly good reason not to start again.

Write out a cheque for the amount that you would spend in the future if you started again. Write the cheque to the tobacco manufacturer of your choice and keep it handy. If you are ever tempted to light a cigarette consider the real cost. *One puff* may cost you more than a year's salary.

Whatever 'enjoyment' there might be in smoking, I doubt it's worth all that!

SELF-REINFORCEMENT

BEGIN TRAINING YOURSELF IN THE ART OF SELF-REINFORCEMENT

Your friends will congratulate you for stopping smoking for a maximum of three days if you're lucky. After that the subject is old hat.

After the three days are up, no one is going to give you much encouragement and so you must do it for yourself.

Only you will know how many cigarettes you didn't smoke.

It is most important to give your new habit of not smoking as much chance as possible by rewarding yourself when you're succeeding.

If you were trying to teach a dog a new trick you would reward it every time it made progress, perhaps by giving it a biscuit or a simple pat or gesture of affection.

Only you will know when you have got yourself through a situation in which you formerly smoked. When you notice give yourself a reward, or at least a mental 'pat on the back'.

Praise yourself for your successes.

Be aware of the improvements to your health and lifestyle. Start a plus list in your notebook of all the benefits you notice – you aren't coughing any more, or you still have breath left at the top of the stairs, or the dark brown 'taste' in the bottom of your mouth when you wake up has gone.

Note the first time someone tells you that you look better, or the time when you first realised you didn't have to worry about your breath smelling.

Or that the ashtrays in your car are now clean, and you never have to worry about asking for an ashtray in a non-smoker's house or office.

You have been drugged most of your adult life; discover what it feels like to be a non-smoking adult. After a short period of detoxification your new vitality will appear.

Reward yourself frequently. Make a special effort to look after yourself and give yourself little treats for the next few weeks.

Develop a sense of self-mastery – each time you notice that you thought of a cigarette but didn't have one, use it as evidence of your ability to succeed in staying off cigs.

Develop a sense of cheerful optimism. Look on the bright

side. It's much more difficult to smoke when you're laughing.

If you are going into situations which you know are going to be difficult, develop a resigned attitude. A couple of hours of uncomfortableness is worth going through to gain the freedom you deserve.

Not only will you feel a lot more confident and proud of yourself if you do suceed in a difficult situation, but you will also find that the next time you are in a similar situation it will be that much easier to cope.

Things will get better.

Just as the physical effects of nicotine withdrawal are temporary, so too the number of thoughts that you have about cigarettes will decline as time passes.

Before I go on to the assignments for this week, and give you a list of things to do should the thoughts of cigarettes get stuck in your head, I want to discuss the most important concept in the whole course, once more.

DECODING

We've suggested in earlier sessions that you smoke on cue to stimuli, either internal or external ones.

Decoding means trying to identify, or analyse what is causing you to think of cigarettes.

Once you have found out why you were thinking of cigarettes in the first place, it is often easier to find a way to get the thought out of your mind.

For instance, some people smoke when they are frustrated. Yet, as you know, lighting up doesn't cure frustration, it's just that you have been accustomed to smoking to relieve any form of discomfort you experience.

When you have identified what was causing you to think of a cigarette, try and think how someone who has never smoked would deal with the situation.

There is a difference between *wanting* a cigarette and *thinking* of one. You can think of sex, or strawberries without rushing off to have them immediately. (Can't you?)

But, in the past, whenever you've *thought* of cigarettes you've lit up. We know now that you don't *want* to smoke, otherwise you wouldn't have spent the last four weeks doing the exercises in the book. Yet you are bound to *think* of cigarettes.

This is a very important distinction to draw.

You don't want to smoke. Yet you are going to think about smoking. So I want you to learn how to deal with the 'thoughts' of smoking when they occur.

When you find yourself thinking of cigarettes this week, try and identify what caused the thought in the first place. Then deal with whatever was causing you to think of smoking in the first place.

I've been told that at Alcoholics Anonymous they have a mnemonic that is useful in determining what caused you to think of smoking.

Their word is **HALT**

H for hungry
A for angry
L for lonely
T for tired

We've added

B for bored
F for frustrated

So the mnemonic now reads **HALT** you Bloody Fool. If you think of a cigarette say to yourself **'Halt you Bloody Fool'**, and try and work out why you were thinking of that cigarette.

Ask yourself:

If I don't want to be a smoker, but I think of cigarettes, what is it that I really want?

Am I hungry?

Lonely?

Bored?

Why am I thinking of a cigarette right now?

What would a non-smoker do in this situation?

Here's a first aid list of things to help you through times when 'thoughts' of cigarettes 'stick' in your mind.

Whatever you do don't smoke until you've tried every step.

1 Breathe deeply and satisfyingly.

2 Don't give in to self-pity. You'll feel a lot better about yourself if you get through the hard times without smoking.

3 Decode. Find out what's causing you to think about smoking and then deal with the situation directly instead of lighting up.

4 Distract yourself. Go into a different room. Take a walk. Do something unusual. Call a friend on the phone. Immerse yourself in some activity that absorbs you completely. DO SOMETHING DIFFERENT.

5 Repattern your life to avoid the most difficult situations. Don't go out with friends who will offer you cigarettes for instance. Avoid heavy drinking sessions, for certain.

6 Refresh yourself – rinse your wrists and ankles under cold running water. Wash your face.

7 Take a warm, relaxing bath.

8 Take some exercise. This helps in several ways. It makes you feel better. It relaxes you. It makes you feel healthier and less likely to want to poison your body. It can make you less irritable. It helps you keep your weight under control.

9 Change the taste in your mouth. Chew on a clove, or some cardamom seed, pickles or lemons.

10 Use a mouthspray.

11 Recite your reasons for wanting to stay off cigarettes. What would you have to 'give up' in order to smoke?

12 Take a sniff of your Butt Jar. Photocopy the label over, and then glue it onto your jar of butt ends that you kept this week.

There are still assignments for you to follow this week. You probably won't remember them unless you re-read this section in a couple of days time. Make a note in your diary to do that NOW.

BUTT JAR

Here lie the remains of the last cigarettes I will ever smoke! May they rest in peace.
BUTT JAR
CUT-OFF DATE:
Instructions: Add ¼ cup water, cover securely and shake. For lowered resolve or when in doubt, remove lid and take a whiff. An instant reminder of smoking's sickening stench and foul filth.
This HabitBreakers souvenir is designed to inspire the protection and preservation of your freedom!
POISON: KEEP OUT OF REACH OF CHILDREN.

ASSIGNMENTS Session Five

Assignment One
Take one day at a time. Try not to think about forever. Take one day at a time, or if necessary take one hour at a time. Don't scare yourself with thoughts of 'forever'.

Assignment Two
Keep a diary. Record your experiences as you are going along – keeping a note of the good times as well as the hard moments. Sometimes simply writing down your difficulties can make life a little more bearable.

Assignment Three
Keep a plus list in the notebook.

Assignment Four
Prepare your butt jar as explained on the label.

Assignment Five
Anticipate malice from some smoking friends and colleagues. Don't let negative friends get the better of you – some smokers will do almost anything to make sure you fail so that they don't feel as bad about their own smoking.

Assignment Six
Start saving the money that you would have spent on cigarettes. Spend it all in three weeks on a present to yourself.

Assignment Seven
Read any information you can find about the risks to your health of smoking. Most smokers don't really know the full extent of the danger of smoking cigarettes – preferring to live in ignorance. Find out the truth.

Assignment Eight
Continue with all past exercises, especially oral gratification, breathing and mirror talk.

Assignment Nine
Don't give in to self-pity.

Assignment Ten
Constantly reinforce your success and reward yourself.

Assignment Eleven
Avoid, or water down, alcohol. Alcohol is likely to have a bigger kick to it during the next couple of weeks so go easy on the drinking. Don't let your resolve weaken because you've had one too many.

Assignment Twelve
Increase your exercise routine another 5 minutes a day.

Assignment Thirteen
DON'T TEST YOURSELF

ONE WILL HURT

NOW FOR THE GOOD NEWS:

One last thing before you put out your final cigarette. Just take a look at the list of medical benefits in store for you in the immediate future.

HEALTH FACTS

The rewards for stopping smoking are both immediate and substantial. The benefits are also cumulative. For example, 10–15 years after quitting, the ex-smoker's risk of premature death is reduced to almost that of the person who has never smoked. And even if you have smoked for many years, you can actually reverse some of the damage by stopping.

These are facts clearly brought out by the Royal College of Physicians' report *Health or Smoking?*, 1983.

(It is estimated that nearly 10 million people in the UK have stopped. Non-smokers now outnumber smokers by 2:1.)

THIS IS HOW YOU'LL BENEFIT:

1. The most immediate benefit is a rapid decline in the level of carbon monoxide in the blood within 12 hours.
2. Your heart and lungs will work more efficiently, and blood will carry more oxygen. This means you'll be less puffed on exertion and have more stamina. You'll be less likely to get asthma attacks. About three-quarters of those who are short of breath notice an improvement very soon after stopping smoking.
3. More than nine out of ten smokers with a chronic cough find the cough disappears or substantially improves in less than a month after stopping smoking. In as many as one in three, the cough and sputum disappear within 2 weeks.

4 The cilia (tiny hairs in the bronchial tubes which become paralyzed in the smoker) begin working again to sweep out germs, mucus and dirt from the lungs. This means you'll be less susceptible to coughs, cold and chest infections.

5 There is less chance of sudden death, a coronary, and chest pain. If you stop smoking following a coronary attack, you'll halve your chance of suffering another. Deaths from coronary heart disease are reduced by two-thirds in the first two years after stopping smoking. (Between 1951 and 1971, many British doctors stopped smoking. During this period the death rate from coronary heart disease amongst doctors fell by six per cent, whereas in a comparable group in the general adult population death rates rose by nine per cent.)

6 Damage to the lungs begins to be repaired almost immediately after quitting. There is actual repair to pre-cancerous lesions, and the normal healthy condition of the lung is restored.

7 The risk of developing lung cancer drops within a few years of stopping. After 10–15 years, the risk approaches that for those who have never smoked.

8 There is also a gradual decrease in the risk of developing cancer of the larynx, mouth, oesophagus, bladder, and pancreas. Ten years after stopping, the risk will be the same as for those who have never smoked.

9 The pulse rate falls, both at rest and after exercise.

10 You will be less tired. You will 'come alive' more quickly in the morning and be more alert during the day.

11 Headaches and stomach-aches which have been caused by smoking will disappear. Eyes will be less irritated.

12 Oral health improves. (Gums stop being 'burned away', no more deposit of nicotine which stains the teeth.)

13 The sense of smell and taste is improved. The absorption of food is better.

14 Skin circulation improves – the complexion starts to look better.

15 If a woman stops smoking before the 20th week of pregnancy, the risk of having a low-weight baby will be similar to that of a non-smoker.

16 Gastric and duodenal ulcers heal quicker and are less likely to come back.

17 You breathe more slowly (i.e. decrease in breathing rate per minute). There is an increase in breathing capacity (i.e. you can take in more air on each breath).

18 You reduce the risk of fire – more fatal fires are caused by cigarettes than by any other source of combustion.

Before I finish this week's session by giving you some suggestions for the following week I want to draw your attention to the list of Secret Weapons – ideas to help you in almost any situation. Use this list if you can't find a solution to a problem.

SECRET WEAPONS

Here's a simple guide to help you handle the problems which you relied on the old cigarette to help you through. The cigarette didn't actually do anything to help. It just gave you something to do while you coped with the problem.

From now, instead of lighting up every time there's a problem, refer to this guide, and see what your options are. And do, of course, come up with your own ideas.

Here we go then . . .

First – Decode and pinpoint the nature of your dissatisfaction.

Second – find an immediate solution in the *Distract* column.

Third – plan a way to *Change* so you won't be caught again.

Decode	Distract	Change
Hungry	Oral Gratification Routine. Mouth Spray.	Read the diet suggestions to repattern your nutrition.

Decode	Distract	Change
Angry/ Frustrated	Deep Breathing. Do some physical exercise, dance to some loud music.	Resolve to avoid source of anger or frustration in future, or change your approach to it.
Lonely	Call or write to a friend. Reward yourself. Visit someone lonelier than you. Do someone a favour.	Become involved with people; make yourself important and available to others.
Tired	Take a break and stretch. Deep breathing. Have some orange juice or soup.	Get enough rest at night. Schedule a nap during the day if you can. Practise yoga. Exercise more regularly.
Bored/Restless	Do something physical. Refer to the Rewards list. Start some project you've been meaning to get into.	Adult Education classes, new hobby. Add some variety to your daily routine.
Indigestion	Take antacid tablet.	Avoid over-eating and highly seasoned foods.
Embarrassed	Remind yourself you're human. Call on your sense of humour.	Don't be so concerned with what others might think of you; they are more concerned with themselves. Rely on your new sense of self-esteem.
Familiar Trigger	Recognise it as a former smoking situation. Observe how non-smokers handle themselves.	Anticipate trigger situations ahead of time – strip them of their power – diffuse their impact.
Self-Pity	Mirror Talk. Try laughter – chances are you're taking yourself too seriously.	Learn to say 'no'. Plan daily rewards.

Decode	Distract	Change
About to Light Up	Deep breathing. Smell your Butt Jar. Smell a smoker. Read your Cancellation of Contract to Be a Smoker at the end of the book. Call a friend.	Review those reasons for stopping. Eliminate self-pity. Nurture your positive attitude. Visit a *HabitBreaker* meeting for reinforcement.
Difficulty Concentrating	Deep breathing. Take a walk. Come back to the task after you've taken a break.	Tackle your tasks during a more productive time of day for you. If the material is boring, try to do something more absorbing.
Tension	Relaxation Ritual. Take a hot shower or bath. Go for a walk or a swim.	Increase Vitamin B1 in form of whole grains or wheat germ. Try to avoid tension or confrontations as much as possible.
Stress/Pressure	Deep breathing. Exercise – diffuse the stress by activating your whole body.	Learn to control your response to stress-producing situations – be flexible, do what's comfortable for you.
Insomnia	Relaxation Ritual. Have a drink of warm milk and honey. Read something supremely boring.	Change the time you go to bed. Don't do any daytime napping. No caffeine after dinner.
Gained Weight	Be mature – consider it a temporary inconvenience for a permanent improvement. Start an exercise programme.	Go on a diet. Repattern your eating as you repatterned your smoking behaviour.

Decode	Distract	Change
Rushed	Take your time, in spite of circumstances. Do deep breathing. Don't be afraid to tell someone you need more time.	Try to start earlier. Anticipate situations that might slow you down, and try to circumvent them or allow time for them.
Feeling Bloated (Fluid Retention)	Put your feet up so they are higher than the rest of your body. Drink water (if reduced salt intake). Approach it positively as a temporary symptom of recovery.	Make yourself knowledgeable about high sodium foods and avoid salt.
Nibbling Too Much	Chew on a ginger root or a clove. Drink water. Oral Gratification Routine.	Study **Food for Thought** (in Session Six, so you won't have filled it in yet) and pinpoint your bad eating habits. Resolve to change them. Restock your kitchen with sensible snacks.
Depressed	Do something physical. Fix yourself up – look your best. Have a good cry, and get it over with. Call someone.	Become involved with people. Check out possibility of water retention. Plan daily rewards.
Worried	Relaxation Ritual. Walk, run – do something physical.	Put problems into perspective. Attack the smallest problem first and resolve it. Take one thing at a time.

Decode	Distract	Change
Disappointed	Mirror Talk. Reward yourself.	Plan an alternative strategy ahead of time, just in case. Accept it with a mature attitude – set a new goal.
Feelings Hurt	Write in your notebook what happened. Read back what you wrote and gain perspective. Give yourself a compensatory treat.	Develop a sense of humour. Try to understand the other person's needs and motivations. Stick pins in a wax model.
Completion of a Pleasurable Event	Count your blessings! Smile at your good fortune. Remind yourself that **one will really hurt you**.	Fully enjoy the 'event' – nothing more is needed.

SUGGESTIONS

- You know that the weeks ahead may be like an emotional roller-coaster but you are prepared.
- You have taken intelligent steps towards eliminating the distress of physical craving and withdrawal symptoms.
- You will not be afraid to live without cigarettes . . . you will not fall apart or break up without a cigarette – remember no one ever died from stopping smoking.
- You have seen into your personal stress and tension periods and have learnt how to relax. You are attempting to develop a calm and serene attitude towards stressful, difficult situations.
- You have proved that you could go without cigarettes in many many different circumstances in which you formerly believed you had to smoke – or else.
- You recognise trigger situations and have the tools you need to beat the habit – with a smile.
- You have learned to handle the thought of a cigarette. If you find yourself thinking of cigarettes try and let the thoughts go without paying much attention to them.
- When you put out that last cigarette tonight, you will command yourself to switch off your desire to smoke – and you will not want to smoke again. Fleeting thoughts may occur but the compulsion will be gone.
- Your success depends upon how much you want to quit.

Stopping smoking has become the most important thing in your life.

- You have come to recognise your own worth.
- You know you can do it.

Go to it.

And enjoy your celebration tomorrow night!

6

6

SESSION SIX

A WEEK WITHOUT SMOKING

Start this session as usual by turning back to Page 33 and filling in your RECORD OF CIGARETTES. This is one of the few courses where 0 is the best grade!

Now comes the hardest part of all for me. The trouble with writing a book instead of being able to engage in conversation is that I can't respond to you personally as I would do in a course.

This means that, even more than in the classes, you're going to have to make sure you can change your attitude by yourself rather than having the guidance of someone able to devote time specifically to you.

One week after I stopped smoking, in fact even after the first day, I was amazed at how easy I was finding the experience.

Over the years, I've spent an enormous amount of time wondering why the courses work for some people but appear not to for others. I hope that the people who have taken our courses will not object too strenuously if I conjecture about the reasons why.

Firstly, most people find the experience of finally stopping, after worrying about it for so long, actually exhilarating. These are the people who have really been looking forward to ending their encounter with cigarettes.

Some of these people have relatively uncomfortable withdrawal symptoms, nonetheless. They deal with them by accepting the physical changes as what they are – temporary inconveniences for the sake of a much improved way of living.

As 'symptoms of recovery' they are actually encouraging signs – signals that you are getting rid of the poisons and returning to normal functioning. A full list of these symptoms and how long they last is included at the end of this chapter.

Some people find the first weeks not quite as easy.

Often they find that the 'thoughts' of cigarettes will simply not go out of their mind. Mostly this group of people will struggle through to the next *HabitBreaker* meeting to get the reinforcement, support and advice that's available in the meetings.

This group of people have *as much chance of succeeding* as the group who are finding it easy. The thoughts do become less frequent if you stick with it.

There is a smaller group of people who have 'one or two' or even more cigarettes during this first week. These people have little chance of stopping smoking completely this time around.

One puff quickly becomes one pack a day. You've wasted all the effort you've put in in the last month if you give in now.

The only chance that this group has, in my opinion (which is frequently wrong) is to do a rapid about face in attitude and *STICK TO IT*.

Here's why I think some people find it easier than others.

They believe in themselves and that they are capable of succeeding.

They may well have tried stopping in some other way before, and rather than totally convince themselves that they can never succeed they become more and more committed to stopping.

The information they receive on the courses rings true, even though not all the subjects are directly related to themselves. They are prepared to accept new ideas and try hard to change the way they think about what cigarettes mean to them.

They make a firm decision to stay off cigarettes for good.

Obviously, you can't expect a book to be able to give the same amount of encouragement as personal contact. Often a good course instructor can really help someone who is genuinely dedicated to succeeding but is having personal problems.

If you don't want to stop smoking you won't find it as easy. If you can find a way of making yourself *want* to stop, you've got the problem licked.

Staying off cigarettes is easy, once you get the hang of it. Firstly, when you think of a cigarette you remember that it is just a thought and that you don't really want to smoke anyway.

Once you've done that the next step is easy too.

Find out why you were thinking of a cigarette at that particular time. Remember HALT You Bloody Fool, and the discomfort theory.

You already know that the cigarette won't affect the outcome of the situation except perhaps as a distraction. If you did light up you'd regret your decision.

It is just a thought, for Heaven's sake!

When you've found out *why* you're thinking of the cig, deal with the situation in some way or other, rather than just waiting for it to go away.

Often it's as simple as forcing yourself to do something different. Distract yourself if necessary.

Read the list of 'Secret Weapons' that I've given you for some helpful hints.

Above all, *just don't smoke*. There's no need to. Whatever you're coming up against will not be any better with cigarettes.

That's how you deal with stray thoughts when they occur.

And you keep on dealing with them in this way until the thoughts occur less and less frequently.

At some time in the future you'll realise that you really have smoked your last cigarette.

From here on our relationship will shift somewhat. Until the day you were to stop smoking, I could simply encourage you to follow those instructions and think about some simple concepts that would enable you to approach stopping smoking from a different perspective.

You have done the real work though.

From here on, it's even more up to you to make best use of the information that I can give you. Good luck!

If you have done everything correctly, this last week may well have been the first week in your adult life that you have not smoked.

That's a tremendous achievement. I hope you are proud of yourself.

No matter how difficult you found this week, if you have not smoked, then you are on your way to saving yourself some £30,000+, improving your looks, your self-esteem and possibly adding years to your life.

Many people find that the first week of not smoking the *HabitBreaker* way is considerably easier than they thought that it would be and are surprised, delighted and amazed at their own success.

Others may well not have found this week so easy.

Some may have been tempted to have 'just the one' that we warned you about at the end of last week's session.

Some people will have succeeded but will still be experiencing uncomfortable symptoms of recovery.

Some people will have noticed dramatic improvements to their health already, and some will be disappointed as the changes that they expected have yet to materialise.

Some people, particularly women, may be concerned that they are overeating, and that their weight gain will mean more risk to their health than smoking.

So the purpose of this week's session is to put your experiences over the past week into perspective, deal with some of the problems, and set you up for the following weeks.

We will be talking mainly about problems, but those of you who found last week a breeze should please read the session anyway – you can never tell when the information will be needed. You may be one of the lucky ones, but often if the first week has been easy, the following week may provide you with some more testing situations. Be prepared anyway.

Start this week's session by filling out the answers on the HOW ARE YOU DOING? form, for your experiences of the last week.

You'll be completing this form at the beginning of the next session so that you'll be able to see the improvements as you get used to your new habit of not smoking. Tick the statements that apply to you each week.

HOW ARE YOU DOING?

WK6/WK7 **Whoopee!**

- ☐ ☐ Big feelings of relief and freedom.
- ☐ ☐ The 'symptoms of recovery' are comforting.
- ☐ ☐ I have complete control in stressful situations.
- ☐ ☐ I'm beginning to feel and look better physically. And it shows!
- ☐ ☐ It's great to be free of smoking.
- ☐ ☐ I 'decode' and then do something about it immediately.

☐ ☐ TOTALS IN THIS CATEGORY.

WK6/WK7 **Don't pin any medals on me yet, but I think I'm going to win**

☐ ☐ Surprised to have gone this long without smoking.
☐ ☐ Surprised I haven't been obsessed with desire to smoke.
☐ ☐ Had a few struggles during the week, but nothing I couldn't handle.
☐ ☐ Getting very proud and less afraid.
☐ ☐ It really didn't hurt and I'm beginning to enjoy the whole experience.
☐ ☐ The 'symptoms of recovery' are only a nuisance, but I know that they are evidence of improvement and that they won't last long.
☐ ☐ Have noticed slight physical improvement – but maybe it's coincidental.
☐ ☐ Sometimes I consciously distract myself when thoughts of smoking enter my mind.
☐ ☐ TOTALS IN THIS CATEGORY.

WK6/WK 7 **Wait for me, I'll catch up soon**

☐ ☐ I haven't smoked all week, but it hasn't been easy.
☐ ☐ I miss my 'old friend' a lot each day and often think how good it would be to have a smoke.
☐ ☐ I feel like a martyr – being deprived of the only real indulgence in my life. What else do I do that's bad?
☐ ☐ Can't say I feel any better than when I smoked, but then I didn't feel bad before I stopped anyway.
☐ ☐ I usually don't do anything to distract, 'decode' or renew my resolve.
☐ ☐ TOTALS IN THIS CATEGORY.

WK6/WK7 **Ugh!**

☐ ☐ Had a few this week – big problems.
☐ ☐ Feel worse than ever, physically (and mentally!).
☐ ☐ Can't seem to get cigarettes off my mind.
☐ ☐ I'd walk a mile for one right now!
☐ ☐ Nothing else seems to 'satisfy' me.
☐ ☐ I really feel like something very precious and special has been taken from me – I generally feel very sorry for myself that I had to stop smoking.
☐ ☐ I've pretty well convinced myself that the weight I've gained is worse than the possibility of lung cancer or emphysema.
☐ ☐ I never 'decode' or distract myself.
☐ ☐ Sometimes I eat food or sweets when I want a cigarette but never do 'oral gratification' to satisfy the need.

☐ ☐ TOTALS IN THIS CATEGORY.

If you have more marks in the first two sections than in the last two sections then you are WINNING. If the reverse is true you must look and see whether it's your overall attitude that needs work.

OK, now for a few more questions. Write down the answers in your DIARY section of your notebook (the section that you should have been writing in each day this week)

1 Was Cut-Off Week easier than doing Week Four's assignments?
2 What is the longest period of waking time you can remember going without thinking of a cigarette?
3 What is your attitude towards yourself and your accomplishments?
4 What symptoms of recovery have you noticed this week?
5 What concept or tool was the most useful to you in getting you over the rough spots?

Next, please tick any of the following that apply to you.

Did you find it?	Yes	Maybe	No
1 Relatively easy	☐	☐	☐
2 Almost constantly difficult	☐	☐	☐
3 Easy at first, then became more difficult	☐	☐	☐
4 Difficult at first, then got easier	☐	☐	☐
5 Have you noticed your cough has gone?	☐	☐	☐
6 Do you feel as though a burden has been lifted from your shoulders?	☐	☐	☐
7 Do you feel tired and muddle-headed – walking into the kitchen only to forget what you wanted?	☐	☐	☐
8 Are you finding the breathing exercise useful?	☐	☐	☐
9 Are you substituting eating instead of oral gratification?	☐	☐	☐
10 Are you starting to feel free?	☐	☐	☐
11 Have you been told that you look better?	☐	☐	☐
12 Do you feel better?	☐	☐	☐
13 About the same?	☐	☐	☐
14 Worse?	☐	☐	☐
15 Do you feel more self-confident and proud?	☐	☐	☐
16 Have you got rewards to look forward to?	☐	☐	☐

If you were taking the course in a group, you would have seen an enormous variety in response. Some people find the first week easy, some, as you will have gathered from the forms above, almost constantly difficult.

It would be preferable if everyone found the experience easy, but experience has shown us that about one-third of people find the first week fairly difficult.

This is not necessarily a bad thing.

Often those who found it easy to stop, also find it easy to start again. They are classic candidates for complacency, saying to themselves: 'Well, if it was that easy to stop, then I can have the odd cigarette when I feel like it.'

If you have tried before to stop smoking then you'll know that 'just one' becomes 'just one pack' before long. You are, as the Americans say, 'A puff away from a pack a day'.

ONE WILL HURT

If you are having difficulties but you are sticking to the course regardless, then I offer you my most sincere congratulations. You *will* find that it will become easier in the weeks ahead.

It takes six weeks to make or break a habit, according to Harvard psychologist William James, and you are only one week into the formation of your new habit of not smoking. If you have smoked for most of your life, you wouldn't expect a completely smooth transition.

It will get easier, do not fear. Even if your week has been a disaster, there must have been times when it was easier than others. All we need to do is make sure that you have more of the times when it was easier, and less time thinking of the problems.

Keep the problem in perspective too. You are currently trying to change one of the most damaging habits to your health that exists. Don't let relatively trivial matters concern you or upset your resolve.

The fact that a third of the population still smokes is evidence that stopping smoking is not as easy as it sounds – if you do succeed you will have accomplished something of immense importance. Do not give up on yourself now.

It may not always be simple to get through the times when you can't stop thinking about cigarettes but *it is possible* – and the more you succeed the easier it is to deal with difficult situations in future.

THERE ARE SOLUTIONS

The three keys to success if you are thinking about cigarettes are:

DECODE. Find what is causing you to think of smoking and do something about it.

DISTRACT. Change your circumstances – do something different.

REPATTERN. If there are particular times of the day or week when not smoking is more difficult, then see if you can change the pattern of your life so as to have fewer of these stressful situations for the time being.

A healthy imagination may be more use to you than anything else. If you are a person with very rigid patterns of behaviour you may find it difficult to imagine yourself doing things in any other way than the one you've been used to even at the expense of your health. I've met many people who have given up on their attempts because they weren't willing to put themselves through any discomfort – seeking justifications and excuses why the course hasn't worked for them – or it was the wrong time or so on. Their rigidity was more important to them than their health.

If you want to succeed you can. All you have to do is not smoke until not smoking has established itself as the normal way of behaviour for you.

If you cheat yourself, thinking you can have one puff here and there, your chances are almost nil.

If you are committed to not smoking, you will treat problems in a different light than if you are merely 'going through the motions'.

You will see even the most dramatic of problems with an attitude of 'Well, if I can get through this half-hour/day/month, then I really will have cracked it.'

If you doubt your own commitment, sooner or later you will find yourself creating excuses or reasons why 'you simply couldn't help yourself.'

There's a world of difference between 'couldn't help yourself' and 'didn't help yourself.'

Truly committed non-smokers simply don't have lighting

up as an option when they are confronted with difficulties.

That's why it is so important to practise the techniques of dealing with 'thoughts' of cigarettes.

If your week was truly terrible, the **CVS to BVS** exercise ought to have stood you in good stead.

It's probably the easiest way of remembering to keep a positive outlook, even in the most dire of situations.

William James said of habits: 'Never let an exception occur 'til the new habit is securely rooted in your life. Each lapse is like letting fall a ball of string which one is carefully winding up; *a single slip undoes more than a great many turns wind up again.*'

Distract yourself and use your imagination to make your own life easier for you while you get used to being a non-smoker.

Sir Richard Bayliss had a particular problem that was causing him to think of cigarettes. Every time he stepped into his surgery in the morning, his secretary would hand him an enormous pile of letters to deal with.

He was used to having a cigarette to help him through his most unpleasant task of the day at a particular time of day. He also discovered, by observing his own behaviour in quite some detail during the course, that he found it difficult to say no to projects that were, in fact, causing him to be even more overworked than he was normally.

His solution, once the problem was clear in his own mind, was simple enough. He started the day with a task that he enjoyed doing, took the letters on when he was in a better frame of mind, and started saying no to the projects that he didn't want.

Not smoking was more important to him than sticking to his established patterns.

He was actually looking after his own life.

Do you have any patterns of behaviour that don't serve you? Do you always react to situations in the same way?

Why not try something different more often.

There is an attitude in our country that doing things for yourself, rather like making money, is somewhat unacceptable. Winning is not really approved of.

Why are we so strict in our own interpretations about what is and what isn't 'done' in our own lives?

We *can* change. We are remarkably adaptable beings.

You must make sure that you get out of life what you want.

Stopping smoking can be an important catalyst in gaining control over your own life.

I have frequently heard smokers say to themselves at the beginning of the course:

'If I can stop smoking I can do anything.'

By observing your own behaviour over the past five weeks you may have noticed certain elements of your life that really don't support you.

This is one reason why some people get really irritable in the period immediately after they have stopped smoking.

Smokers can act as martyrs – because they fear that because they aren't able to stop smoking there must be something wrong with them, they tend to put themselves down and find fault with their own actions.

Suddenly they kick the smoking habit and their ideas about themselves change – rapidly. They are no longer willing to put up with some of the elements in their lives that depress or upset them – and this unusual standing up for themselves can appear to their friends and colleagues as a change for the worse – they are irritable, outspoken and so on.

Frankly, I think this change is a good thing. It is true that your sense of self-esteem will increase when you have mastered not smoking – and this effect should spill out into other areas. If, having stopped smoking, you start to challenge the relevance of other parts of your life – all well and good.

The trouble is that, like a small child who has just learnt to ride a bicycle and wants the whole world to know about it, new ex-smokers can go over the top in their efforts to re-arrange their lives, often to the detriment of all concerned.

If, having dealt with one area of your life that doesn't work (smoking), you want to improve other areas, do take your time and think about the effect that your actions are having on others. They may not share your current enthusiasm for putting change into effect.

WARNING

If you really are stuck in your thinking and consider that, despite anything that may have been said or discovered in the weeks prior to cutting off, an object of great value has been taken from you and you are now missing your old friend, then unless you can achieve a turn-around in your own attitude to the subject, your chances of remaining off cigarettes are next to nothing.

Consider what you are *really* 'giving up'.

During the fourth week, if you followed the assignments, you will have found that smoking on its own is fairly boring and frustrating. It is only the association with other elements of living that make smoking enjoyable.

What is so brilliant about sticking a tube of vegetable matter into your mouth, setting fire to it, and then breathing in poisonous and carcinogenic smoke?

Do you really think that the 'enjoyment' you think that you might get from lighting up a cigarette is worth all the negative effects that being a smoker entails? (Including the

£30,000 plus that you'll be paying to the tobacco manufacturer of your choice and to the Government in taxes.)

Of course you don't.

YOU MUST LOOK AT STOPPING SMOKING AS A GIFT THAT YOU ARE GIVING YOURSELF, NOT A PUNISHMENT

It is much easier when you have totally and utterly decided that you will not smoke again. Then you don't have to worry about *whether* or not you might have one anymore, just how are you going to deal most constructively with the situation in which you are 'thinking' of a cigarette.

And, the more success that you put under your belt the more your confidence will grow.

Keep concentrating on any good aspects of not smoking that you can find that apply to you, and see if you can find alternative, imaginative ways of dealing with current problems.

Success will come if you set your mind to it.

Let me recap the 'Guidelines for Maintaining Your Non-Smoking' habit.

1 Re-read your notebook.

2 Continue to reward yourself.

3 Do not take a puff. **ONE WILL HURT.**

4 Don't be complacent.

5 Be patient. Some changes may occur more slowly than you would have wanted.

And, of course, don't forget to

DECODE, DISTRACT AND REPATTERN.

Remember to ask yourself:

'If I think I want a cigarette, but I no longer wish to be a smoker, what is it that I really want?'

WEIGHT

Probably the most common excuse for returning to smoking is that the would be non-smoker puts on weight.

So, let's first of all try and understand how putting on weight could be a problem.

There are three areas of interest:

Firstly, smokers are used to giving their mouths plenty of stimulus. Drawing ten puffs per cigarette on twenty cigarettes a day means performing the sucking movements of smoking at least two hundred times a day.

Stopping giving your mouth this attention with the cigarettes, and replacing it instead with eating means weight gain galore.

So teaching yourself to give your mouth attention in other ways than calories is one way.

Mouthwashes, the oral gratification routine, moving your lips around to stimulate the salivary glands, chewing unsweetened chewing gum, pickles, lemons and cloves all help to give your mouth the attention that it has been used to.

Secondly, many people, but women in particular, suffer from a *temporary* increase in water retention, contributing a few pounds in weight gain.

If you are feeling bloated, if the rings on your fingers have become tight, or your ankles or wrists have swollen, then you are probably feeling the effects of water retention.

There is no clear-cut understanding as to why this increase in retention should occur, but there are well known practices that can ease the effects.

Avoid high sodium foods for a while. These include anything containing monosodium glutamate (a flavouring used in most Chinese cooking) and any food with a heavy salt content.

Keep a watch on how much salt you are using on your food.

Choose foods that are natural diuretics such as asparagus, parsley, horseradish, rhubarb, strawberries and melons.

Drink plenty of fresh water.

If the symptoms persist, go and see your doctor.

Thirdly, when you give up smoking, a small change occurs in your body's metabolism.

On average a smoker's heart will beat six or seven beats more per minute than a non-smoker's. That's ten thousand beats more every day. Your metabolism is speeded up by the stimulant effect of the cigarette.

When you stop smoking, your heart rate will tend to fall, as will your basic metabolic rate. What this means in practice is that you will tend to put on a small amount of weight unless you take some corrective action.

You have two choices available to you if you want to remain at a similar weight. Either eat fewer calories, or expend more calories by taking more exercise.

Losing weight is more easily talked about than achieved. There are so many conflicting views, diets and regimes available, some of which seem to work for some people but not for others. If you do have problems keeping your weight down, you will probably have read more on this subject than I have.

My own personal preference is to increase the amount of exercise (provided that there is no medical reason against).

I find that not only does it help me control my weight, it also makes me feel good (which is not something I can say for any diet I have been on). I feel fitter mentally and physically after a good run, or game of tennis, sail etc.

In the first couple of weeks after quitting, many people find that they are eating slightly more. It takes a massive weight gain before the danger to health from being overweight approaches that of being a smoker.

Provided that the extra eating isn't excessive and if it is helping you cope at the moment without smoking, then eat a bit more. You can always tackle your weight gain later, using the guidelines.

Don't use putting on weight as a justification for resuming smoking.

Ask yourself some questions before you put food into your mouth.

Have I eaten in the last four hours?

Is it my mouth or my stomach that is hungry?

If you decide that your mouth needs attention then stimulate it in one of the ways we've already mentioned.

If it is your stomach that wants the attention, ask yourself whether the breathing exercise would provide any relief. You'll remember that we talked about a deep drag on a cigarette being one of the times that you use your diaphragm correctly.

If you decide that you are really hungry after all, choose to eat the right sorts of food. You know what they are.

Answer the questions about your eating habits to see if there are any changes that you'd like to make. Some weight control guidelines follow.

FOOD FOR THOUGHT

	YES / OFTEN	SOME TIMES	NO / RARELY
1 *Do you feel you should eat everything on your plate?*			
2 *Do you have seconds?*			
3 *Is your meal schedule irregular?*			
4 *Do you eat a meal standing up?*			
5 *Do you keep nuts, biscuits, crisps, sweets, etc, handy?*			
6 *Do you eat while watching TV?*			
7 *Do you eat ice cream or popcorn at the movies?*			
8 *Do you carry chewing gum and/or mints with you?*			
9 *Do you munch or chew gum when you drive?*			
10 *Do you drink fizzy soft drinks?*			
11 *Do you have more than one alcoholic drink before dinner?*			
12 *Do you eat when you read or study?*			

13 *Do you eat in bed?*			
14 *Do you have an alcoholic drink before bed?*			
15 *Do you wake up and raid the refrigerator?*			
16 *Do you nibble when you get angry or feel depressed?*			
17 *Do you nibble when you have an unpleasant thing to do?*			
18 *Do you eat when you're bored?*			
19 *Do you think some people are happier when they're fat?*			
20 *Do you get angry when someone suggests you shouldn't nibble?*			
21 *Do you hide snacks and goodies in secret places?*			
22 *Are you uneasy if your secret places aren't stocked?*			
23 *Do you get angry if someone eats your 'hidden' snacks?*			
24 *Do you salt your food before tasting it?*			
25 *Do you gulp your food?*			
26 *Do you eat on cue to external stimuli such as the sight of pastry?*			
27 *Do you skip breakfast?*			
28 *Do you skip lunch?*			
29 *Do you skip dinner?*			
30 *Do you eat 'take away' foods (pizzas, hamburgers etc)?*			
31 *Do you ever shop for food when you are hungry?*			

32 *Do you feel you have to finish the children's leftovers?*			
33 *Do you make secret visits to the larder?*			
ADD EACH COLUMN			

We consider each yes a poor eating habit. If you want optimum health we suggest you try to change each 'Yes' to a 'Sometimes' or 'Rarely'.

WEIGHT CONTROL GUIDELINES

1 Remove from your home entirely – or move to a less convenient location – all foods that can be eaten without preparation, i.e. potato crisps, sweets, biscuits, raisins, cakes, etc.

2 At mealtime: serve from the stove, not the table; use a smaller plate; fill your plate only once; and pause and lay down your utensils after each bite. Eat more slowly – allow time for the food you've eaten to reach your stomach before taking another bite. Or, try eating with chopsticks for a while. It may be awkward, but it will slow you down.

3 Before you begin each meal, picture yourself as slender. Eat only as much as is necessary, not as much as is available. Habit occurs with eating as well as smoking. You are not required to start at the appetizers and eat through eight courses to dessert and beverage. You can survive very satisfactorily, and even more comfortably, with far less food than you think.

4 Never eat when doing anything else, such as reading or watching TV, nor at any place other than your dining table.

5 If you feed children, don't pick at their leftovers. Be cold-blooded and throw them out – or, if untouched, recycle for later use.

6 Engage in pleasurable alternative activities whenever you get the urge to eat between meals. Take a walk . . . or a bike ride, or call a 'positive' friend.

7 Repattern your movements to bypass sources of food. Take a route that cuts out the shop where you usually stop for nibbles; avoid food vending machines; get out of the house when you might normally raid the pantry, etc.

8 Activate the oral gratification kit when the urge to nibble occurs. Oral gratification is doubly important in weight control. Put a bottle of mouthwash in the refrigerator. When you open the door, rinse your mouth with the pleasantly cold mouthwash. It will remove the 'expectation of food' sensation from your mouth. It also gives you the satisfaction of opening the refrigerator door, taking something out, and putting it in your mouth.

9 Get a 'dream picture' of someone that looks like you or the way you would like to look and tape it to your mirror, refrigerator or bread bin.

10 Keep a notebook: record everything you eat for one week. You must begin to be completely **aware** of every speck you put into your mouth.

11 Eat only when hungry! Don't eat on cue to any outside stimulus such as a TV commercial, or the sight of a pastry in the bakery window; nor as a response to an emotional discomfort such as anger or anxiety. Recognise your eating triggers and repattern.

12 Once again, examine self-pity very carefully. Reward yourself frequently in small ways – **PAMPER YOURSELF**. Consider rewards for yourself that are not food – a leisurely bath; a half-hour to read for pleasure; browsing in an antique shop; puttering in the garden, or with sports equipment, or in the workshop, etc.

Next week's session is the last. If you are like the great majority of people who come on our courses, you probably didn't do many of the assignments last week.

Please make a determined effort to complete them this week – after all it's the last time you'll have to do them.

ASSIGNMENTS Week Six

Assignment One
Develop your awareness of improvements, to your health and otherwise, and continue your 'PLUS LIST' that you've been keeping in your notebook.

Assignment Two
Look for articles about smoking? Has there been anything in the news recently?

Assignment Three
Be grateful in situations when you can't smoke.

Assignment Four
Continue putting aside the money you've been spending on cigarettes. Plan to spend it on *you* to celebrate your success.

Assignment Five
Make a list of future trigger situations.

Assignments Six and Seven
Continue observing both smokers and non-smokers to see how they behave.

Assignment Eight
Tell other people how pleased you are now that you've stopped.

Assignment Nine
Continue with all past exercises especially oral gratification, breathing exercises and **CVS to BVS**.

Assignment Ten
DON'T TEST YOURSELF. ONE WILL HURT!

Assignment Eleven
Take one day at a time.

Assignment Twelve
Don't feed your face.

Assignment Thirteen
Include more rewards in your life.

Assignment Fourteen
Limit alcohol for a while until you are *totally* comfortable with drinking and not smoking.

SUGGESTIONS

- You are becoming aware of your increased capacity for dealing with other problems of living.
- You are aware of your new, improved self-image and like yourself more.
- You are becoming more calm and relaxed.
- You are starting to become confident and have more self-esteem. You are starting to be master of yourself.
- *You won't let a 'thought' of a cigarette get stuck in your head.*
- You are enjoying your new freedom.

One more thing and a most constructive habit to begin. Each night, as you turn off the light and pull the covers over you, review the day and say; 'No matter what happened today. It was a good day . . . at least I didn't smoke.'

SYMPTOMS OF RECOVERY

SYMPTOM	AVERAGE DURATION	TREATMENT
DIGESTIVE **ACID INDIGESTION/HEARTBURN**		
The most common digestive problem. The paradox here is smokers who had acid indigestion while they smoked, find it disappears; smokers who never had acid indigestion often become troubled with it after they quit.	3 weeks to 3 months. Not the same intensity throughout.	Natural mineral water for mild acid indigestion; stronger proprietaries if necessary. Reduction or elimination of acid producing foods such as caffeine, chocolates and other greasy heartburn producing items.

NAUSEA

A very infrequent reaction.	1 to 2 weeks. Occasional reports of a day or two of intermittent nausea.	Any usual treatment or just put up with it – it will pass.

DIARRHOEA

Smokers frequently feel they have a virus or the '24-hour bug.'	Several days in most cases.	Common sense. Temporarily cut down intake of orange juice and fresh fruits and vegetables.

CONSTIPATION

Rare but of great concern for those who have a history of constipation. Experience shows this to be a rare but serious problem. When someone approaches you with this problem very confidentially, don't treat it lightly. This one may not go away and may need treatment by an understanding physician. The risk here is a physician who will prescribe 'start to smoke again' as the treatment.	Several weeks to several months.	Use all treatment as prescribed by your doctor in the past. Pay special attention to your diet. If of long duration, speak to your doctor. Nicotine as a drug triggers the bowels in some cases. There are other natural means which can achieve the same results.

FLATULENCE

	Generally several weeks at most. However, a few reported cases of extended duration.	Patience. It will soon pass. Temporarily avoid gas producing food and drinks.

RESPIRATORY

Generally all gagging coughs, throat clearings, chest tightness and other related respiratory problems disappear very dramatically within the first several weeks. These too are Symptoms of Recovery. The following have been reported as occurring after cessation to people who never had these problems before.

PHLEGM

This requires constant clearing of the throat and is probably attributable to the awakening of the cilia now that nicotine no longer paralyzes it – a very good sign indeed. It may also be caused by the new natural activity of the nasal passages.	A few days to a few months.	Something hot to drink, gargles, lozenges that cut phlegm, time.

HOARSENESS

Similar to above. Many reported cases.	Several weeks to several months.	The same as for phlegm except use soothing lozenges.

SINUS CONGESTION

This is both a respiratory and a soft tissue condition. A substantial number of people find their old sinus conditions erupt for a period of time shortly after Cut-Off.	A few days to a few months.	Management by physician or self-treatment as indicated.

COUGH

Due to reactivated cilia.	1–2 weeks.	Gratitude. The body is restoring itself.

CIRCULATORY

HEIGHTENED AWARENESS AND DIZZINESS

This may be a reaction to the improved circulation and increased oxygen to the brain, now that blood vessels are no longer being constricted by nicotine.	Few days (unless caused by low blood pressure).	Good judgement. Rest. Orange juice. Time to readjust to the normal complement of oxygen in your blood.

LEG PAINS

Improved circulation seems to show itself as cramps in the most commonly affected parts – the legs.	Several weeks.	Elevate the legs, massage, good common sense, time.

SWELLING/BLOATING

Generally, a result of fluid retention due to decreased caffeine (a diuretic) and the counter reaction of nicotine withdrawal which itself is *not* a diuretic. Swelling can also be caused by changes in the circulatory process – more blood entering extremities which in the past were deprived because of poor circulation.	Several days to several weeks.	Doctor may prescribe mild diuretic. Increase exercise, reduce salt intake. Time. Elevate the legs to stimulate the elimination of fluids.

STIFFNESS

See also Leg Pains and Swelling above. Stiffness may be also associated with temporary muscular changes. Relationships of muscular changes to quitting is still little understood.	A few days to a few weeks.	Warm baths. Patience.

TINGLY FINGERS

Due to improved circulation.		Patience.

MISCELLANEOUS

DROWSINESS **MUDDLE-HEADEDNESS** **FATIGUE** **SLEEPINESS/LETHARGY**	2–3 weeks	Orange juice, breathing exercise. Cat naps when possible. Physical exercise to stimulate circulation.

INSOMNIA

		Deep breathing. Warm milk and honey. Also, you may require less sleep due to quitting. Many people can function beautifully on 4 to 5 hours sleep.

BLEEDING GUMS

	4–8 weeks	See a dentist.

7

7

SESSION SEVEN

TIME TO REVIEW PROGRESS

Congratulations! Two weeks without smoking should give you a tremendous feeling of pride and self-confidence.

Enter your zeros into the RECORD OF CIGARETTES on Page 33.

Cast your mind back six weeks ago to the beginning of the course – and spend a couple of minutes taking in your success.

The purpose of this last session is for you to really grasp the magnitude of your achievement, and to focus on your future as a non-smoker.

We'll be looking back at some of the forms that you filled in at the first session to see how much your health has improved, and how many of the Reasons for Stopping you have achieved.

I'll show you an example of the Contract you unwittingly signed when you started smoking, listing all the indignities and burdens that smokers have to put up with, and you'll have a chance to cancel that contract once and for all.

Although I promised not to scare you with any horror stories about the perils of smoking, I think it's useful reinforcement now that you've stopped smoking.

So we'll go through a quick summary of the current evidence about the dangers of smoking. You'll find it encouraging and extremely reinforcing to become familiar with health problems you should now not face.

Most of all, though, I want to get over the information that I think is most useful in helping you stay off cigarettes *for ever*.

And if you're still experiencing quite a few problems, I hope to be able to give you some more useful hints.

We'll take a short look at future trigger situations that might start you thinking about lighting up again with a view to forewarning you.

But let's start as always by completing the paperwork.

Fill in the HOW ARE YOU DOING? form again that you first saw last week. Take a look at how your feelings have changed over the past two weeks as you have learnt to deal with more and more situations.

Remember that remarks in the top two categories are evidence of your success, remarks in the other two show you areas in which you still need to keep some attention.

Turn back to Page 145 and complete that right away.

Two weeks after I'd stopped, I was still finding it easy, though some of the 'high' of success was wearing off. Nevertheless, by this stage I had convinced myself that I was not ever going to smoke again.

If you are still finding it difficult to adjust *your* attitude, then I have one last tip and suggestion.

Choose to have your experience become easier. Simply tell your own mind to stop bothering you with petty problems – you have decided to stop – and that's that.

Accept any difficult times with an almost resigned attitude but rejoice every time you get a chance to reinforce the good side of stopping smoking.

Ask yourself, over and over again:

What do I really want for myself?

To be a smoker or a non-smoker?

If you want to be a non-smoker, which you certainly do if you have got this far with the course, then stick with it. It will get easier if you eliminate the idea of lighting up being a possible solution to any situation.

Close your mind to any possibility of ever having a cigarette, grit your teeth through the bad moments and keep an eager eye out for things that you want to do for yourself to enhance your own life.

Let's go back to the first session and review the WHAT YOU PUT UP WITH form (Page 23). Answer the twenty questions again and note which ones have changed in the two short weeks you have not been smoking.

Are any in the process of change?

While it may take several years for your lungs to become totally clean, almost all the noticeable improvements to your health will appear a short while after you've stopped.

We heard the good news about the changes to your health that stopping smoking brings in the last session. I promised not to scare you with the bad news about the dangers of smoking – at least until after you'd stopped smoking.

Many smokers know that smoking is dangerous but, because of what they perceive as their inability to stop smoking, they avoid becoming too familiar with the actual level of risk.

It came as a surprise to me, for example, to know that *one in four* young male smokers will be killed by smoking related diseases.

I thought it was just something that happened to the 'bloke next door'.

Having quit smoking myself, I found it valuable to know the extent of the risks – it was helpful for me to reinforce my resolve. After all, our biggest problem is complacency.

So I've included what I see as the most relevant parts of the *Report on Smoking and Health* published by the Royal College of Physicians to inform you.

HEALTH FACTS

1 Tobacco accounts for some 15–20 per cent of all British deaths. (At an annual death rate of about 100,000 this means that about 275 people die every day from smoking-related diseases.)

2 One in four young male smokers will be killed by smoking-related diseases, and a smoker of 20 cigarettes a day will lose about five or six years of life.

3 Smoking is a primary cause of lung cancer, chronic bronchitis and emphysema, coronary heart disease, and circulatory diseases. It is also a cause of cancer of the tongue, larynx, oesophagus, pancreas and bladder; also, miscarriage, still birth, neonatal death and stomach ulcer. It makes asthma worse, and can be harmful to those with high blood pressure.

4 Sickness due to cigarette smoking leads to the loss of an estimated 50 million working days each year (about four times the loss due to strikes). People who smoke more than 20 cigarettes a day have twice as much time off work because of illness as do non-smokers.

5 A pack-a-day smoker takes more than 70,000 puffs a year. Each time the smoke is inhaled, all the carbon monoxide, over 90 per cent of the nicotine and 70 per cent of the tar are retained.

6 Carbon monoxide reduces the oxygen-carrying capacity of the blood by as much as ten per cent. This is what causes shortness of breath upon exertion.

7 The pack-a-day smoker inhales in the smoke, about a full cup of tar – eight ounces – every year. (To appreciate the volume and quality of tar, think of a jar of molasses.)

8 If you injected a man of average weight with one drop of nicotine (which is roughly the equivalent amount of nicotine found in three packs of cigarettes of the strength of Marlboro or Kent) he would die within a few minutes.

Additional Points of Interest

- The tobacco industry spends over £100 million a year on promotion and advertising.
- In 1982/83, smokers paid about £4,200 million in tobacco taxes.
- Smoking costs the NHS more than £150 million a year.

Now let's go over last week's assignments.

1 Develop your awareness of improvements, to your health and otherwise and continue your 'PLUS LIST' that you've been keeping in your notebook.

2 Look for articles about smoking? Has there been anything in the news recently?

3 Be grateful in situations when you can't smoke.

4 Continue putting aside the money you've been spending on cigarettes. Plan to spend it on *you* to celebrate your success.

5 Make a list of future trigger situations.

How many of these did you get down?

■ **Specific routines**
Emerging from a department store or movie theatre
A break at a meeting
Waiting rooms
Intermission at a performance
Embarking on a plane trip
'No Smoking' sign goes off
Riding in a taxi cab
Sedentary competition–chess, bridge, poker, scrabble, backgammon, etc.
Waiting for your turn to bowl
Car breaks down
Stuck in traffic
All-night vigil at the hospital

■ **Seasonal events**
First swim of the season
First ski run of the season

Spring cleaning
Out on the boat, fishing
Golf tournament, tennis, etc.
Queuing at post office during Christmas rush
Filing Income Tax Return
Wedding reception
Attending a football game
Waiting in physician or dentist's office for an examination
Mowing the lawn, raking leaves
Shovelling snow off the walk
Home being painted
Final exams/Qualifying exams

■Adrenalin-pumping situations
Automobile accident
A child in danger
Robbery/burglary/mugging
Rescuing a victim
Fire
Escape from danger
Winning the pools/Premium Bonds
Good news/bad news/no news

■Emotional triggers
Self-pity
Disillusionment
Did poorly on an exam
A fight with a loved one
Financial setback
Learning of a serious illness
Failure
Fighting a deadline
Balancing the checkbook
Request for a raise turned down
Boredom
Loss of job (retired/fired)
Job interviews
Loss of a loved one
Loss of a big order
Fear of unknown–an operation, new job, move to another city
Feeling inadequate

Kept waiting by someone
Success (end of striving)
Loss of a pet
Loss of precious property
Loneliness
Ailing parent comes to live with you
Kids move away from home

■Physical triggers

Accident resulting in pain
Resting after biking up a hill
Holiday fragrances (Christmas, Thanksgiving, etc.)
Subliminal messages
A strain of music that's tied to a former smoking response
No heat in winter, very cold
No air in summer, very hot and stuffy
Personal encounter with someone you used to smoke with
Consumed too much alcohol
Stimulants (from coffee to pep pills and beyond)

■Social triggers

Attending a big party
Terminating a personal relationship
Being the only one not invited
Being snubbed
The boss and wife are coming to dinner
Being a stranger in town
Embarrassed by a faux pas
Someone you just met offers you a cigarette–your former brand
Stood up for a date
Cancelling the wedding
Spilled red wine on your hostess's heirloom lace tablecloth
Friend who smokes moves in for a month
First time you have a houseful of smoking guests
Showing off, complacent–bragging one can't hurt, you've got it made

Any one of these situations could perhaps cause one to think of a cigarette. But the price of one cigarette is a full-blown smoking habit, a price we can't afford. It would be self-defeating to smoke in response to any one of these situations. Instead of having one problem, you'd then have two problems.

Whenever confronted by a cigarette-thought-producing-trigger, invoke your secret weapon, the phrase that's become a conditioned response . . .

SMOKING DOESN'T MAKE ANYTHING BETTER!

6/7 Continue observing both smokers and non-smokers to see how they behave.
8 Tell other people how pleased you are now that you've stopped.
9 Continue with all past exercises especially oral gratification, breathing exercises and **CVS to BVS**.
10 **DON'T TEST YOURSELF**.
11 Take one day at a time.
12 Don't feed your face.
13 Include more rewards in your life.
14 Limit alcohol for a while until you are *totally* comfortable with drinking and not smoking.

How well did *you* do the assignments last week?

Probably not too well, going by the willingness of people in our courses to do the assignments *after* they've stopped actually putting smoke into their lungs.

You may be different, of course.

If you can follow these assignments for a couple of weeks more, the chances of you returning to smoking are slim. I suggest that you re-read this chapter, and the previous one once a week for the next month or so.

The most often recorded reason why people who have taken our courses resume smoking is because they become complacent and think that they can have 'just one'.

YOU CAN'T.

ONE WILL HURT

The most certain route to staying off cigarettes for good is actually very simple.

Decide that you won't ever smoke again. And then don't.

On the following few pages are the common 'booby-traps' that people fall into and resume smoking. Take a good look at them.

CAREFUL
OR
I WILL
RETURN

Session Seven

BOOBY-TRAPS

As you move about in the world as a non-smoker, you want to be careful to avoid the traps and hazards that create excuses for starting again. If you know where they lie, you can circumvent them.

Here are the danger signs to watch for:

1 Complacency

You quickly forget the discomforts of smoking . . . the difficulty of stopping. The mind has a convenient memory and remembers only the good aspects of smoking.

A smoker may con himself into believing that he's 'got it made'. Once past the direct activity of stopping, it's easy to say 'one won't hurt' and then, according to reports, somehow, over the weeks, 'one' has become 'one pack a day!' One chink in the wall of your resolve begins erosion of the wall. A study several years ago by Dr Donald T. Fredrickson, then of the NY City Board of Health, revealed that 15 out of 25 recidivists (people who start smoking again) resumed smoking because of complacency.

Don't ever take for granted your hard-earned freedom!

2 Alcohol
Nothing softens the resolve like alcohol. The danger is not the cocktail party as a trigger situation but that marginal excess which strips you of control and allows rationalisations to swarm. The 'high' when one is apt to say, 'What the hell . . . I won't worry about it tonight.' Avoid heavy drinking until you have stabilised your attitude and begun to enjoy not smoking.

3 Weight
Those people who view stopping smoking as a form of self-denial and reach for food as a substitute, are creating an excuse to start again. An increase in weight is viewed by the mature person as another challenge or project which will be managed at the right time. Weight, in itself, does not create cravings for a cigarette. All too often we hear that people who resumed smoking because they gained weight found themselves saddled with the double problem of being overweight smokers.

4 Physiological problems
People who have become impatient with a sometimes lingering Symptom of Recovery – such as muddle-headedness, drowsiness, constipation – forget that they are temporary and transient. Consider how long and how much one smoked – everything cannot disappear overnight. BE PATIENT. The body will restore itself. Keep perspective. Is the danger and misery of the smoking habit a fair trade-off for one annoying Symptom of Recovery?

5 Personal problems
There will always be personal problems. Life is like that. To smoke in the face of a personal problem is counterproductive. Instead of one problem, you'll have two problems. *There are no reasons for smoking . . . only excuses*. Remember: ***Smoking never made anything better.***

6 'My spouse/lover/friend/whoever started'

A person with whom you share your life has started smoking. . . 'It's hard' . . . or 'Cigarettes are always around me now' . . . etc. Would you use that person's toothbrush? Then don't smoke that person's cigarettes – they're not yours. We are all free to make our own choices. You have chosen not to smoke. It is your choice to be free.

7 'Smoking never lost its charm for me'

Do you recognise any self-deception in that one? Or, 'I just wanted to see how it tasted', or, 'I missed the taste'. Too bad! We agreed cigarettes tasted lousy.

8 Boredom

For many people loneliness and boredom are the core of their universe. A cigarette becomes their only friend and the only sparkle of life and excitement that they seem to be able to generate for themselves. The tragedy is that in this busy world, which needs human contribution, only the bedridden might be forgiven for being bored. So . . . set new goals and make the most of yourself – improve yourself with new skills and knowledge. Make yourself important to other people. Become involved.

9 Spite

When pressures pile up – the world seems against you, the boss is impossible, the spouse or kids for whom you stopped give you a hard time – a natural reaction is: 'I'll show him (her/them)' . . . 'I'll have a cigarette. Look at the sacrifice I made in stopping and this is the thanks I get . . . I'll smoke one just for spite!' TO SPITE WHOM? Case histories show this spirals down to a big case of 'poor me' and results in SELF-PITY. This is one of the prime reasons for insisting you have a genuine desire to stop – not for your family or anyone else.

10 Ignorance in switching

Smokers like to persuade themselves that there are 'safe' cigarettes . . . 'less hazardous' pipes or cigars. *HabitBreakers* know that this is simply NOT TRUE. Dr Alton Ochsner, when asked about the safety of other forms of smoking, replied: 'It remains with the smoker to choose the site of his cancer': i.e. ANY CIGARETTE OR TOBACCO PRODUCT IS SAFE UNTIL YOU LIGHT IT.

11 Completion of the pleasurable cycle
Here is a specific application of complacency at work under totally non-threatening, comfortable circumstances.

When one has finished a particularly good meal; when one is surrounded by good friends (who may or may not be smoking) etc, one has a sudden feeling of wanting to do that 'one more thing' to make the whole situation perfect – the Completion of the Pleasurable Cycle.

It isn't the car accident or the argument with the boss or teenage son, or the sudden, acute business problem that is the culprit – but, rather, a comfortable, pleasant occasion during which one feels no real concern.

The important thing to remember is that the pleasurable events cannot be enhanced by smoking – rather they will be marred by the guilt and anger you'll feel for lighting up.

12 The lack of self-worth
For one who has developed self-confidence and a strong sense of self-worth as a result of stopping smoking, the chances of starting again are very slim. Get to know yourself finally as an adult, accept your limitations and strengths, feel comfortable with yourself, and don't make excuses for your actions any longer. You have achieved something of value . . . you have earned your own respect! This is maturity which is based on self-respect. The thought of taking a cigarette represents the loss of personal dignity and freedom. Viktor E. Frankl, writing of his concentration camp experience, wrote in his book, *Man's Search for Meaning*:

'Everything can be taken away from a man but one thing: the last of the Human Freedoms – to choose one's attitude in any given set of circumstances – to choose one's own way!'

CHOOSE TO ENJOY NOT SMOKING!

Each of the above causes for starting again is a possible chink in your armour. If lack of resolve finds a tiny crack it will break through and cause your new freedom some real problems.

When your reasons to be free of the habit are strong, your *motivation* is your armour. *Nothing* can penetrate it – no seductive memory of your lost 'love' . . . no stressful situation . . . no complacency . . . ***nothing!***

When the benefits and pleasures of not smoking exceed any benefit or pleasure you thought smoking gave you, you will be really free. That's why those of us who are liberated are confident we'd never want to smoke again. We'd feel like we were losing something of great value. It's such a pleasure not to smoke.

So, the secret of success is building onto your reasons for being glad you don't smoke any more; strengthening your *motivation*, every day, at every opportunity. Then nothing can ever make you take that first cigarette!

CONGRATULATIONS ON NOT SMOKING!

On the next page is a copy of the contract that you signed when you started smoking.

Take a good look at it, and then fill in your details where appropriate.

WELL DONE!

OFFICIAL CANCELLATION OF MY CONTRACT TO BE A SMOKER

I,————, having been of sound body, but of unenlightened mind, AGREED at the tender age of———years to BECOME A SMOKER: i.e. TO BUY, CATER TO, AND CONSUME CIGARETTES (CIGARS, PIPES) every day, for the rest of my life:

I further agreed, in fulfilment of the above contractual obligation, to abide by the tenets, requirements and obligations imposed on me by the manufacturers, advertisers, and purveyors of the Tobacco Industry . . . to crave nicotine, continually (in ever increasing amounts), to suffer the agony of abrupt withdrawal – be it voluntary or involuntary, to resort to the humiliating practice of re-igniting butts in cases of over-accelerated consumption; to sustain an annoying, hacking, persistent cough; to surrender a diurnal quota of phlegm orchestrated by frequent throat-clearings; to suffer red, itchy, burning eyes, pounding or ringing in ears, parched nasal membranes and a dry sore throat. A tight, uncomfortable feeling in my chest, while ever present, should only cause severe discomfiture when running, coughing, laughing, or engaging in other physical activities, the pain from which to be only brief in duration due to the self-protective mechanism of becoming easily winded in the execution of the above mentioned exertions. Other such physical burdens include nicotine-stained fingers and upper lip, smoker's 'odour' of body, hair and clothes, and offensive smoker's breath that need be camouflaged by mouthwashes, breath sprays, toothpaste, gum, sweets, and mints, precipitating accelerated tooth decay resulting in costly dental rehabilitation – to wit, fillings, crowns, and dentures, plus a respectful distance from non-smoking interlocutors. Acid indigestion. Headaches. Trembling hands, sometimes unduly perspiring. Occasional numbness in fingers, toes, arms, legs, and unaccountable tingly sensations. Possible vision impairment. Sulphur match burns, torn skin from lower lip, singed eyelashes.

I further agreed to perform the blind ritual of smoking one cigarette before retiring, followed by a self-imposed awakening for a nocturnal fix, and to light up one more to start my heart pumping in the morning.

I have agreed that material possessions are unimportant and that to deface or destroy other people's possessions as well as my own with cigarette burns is not intentionally malevolent, only careless. To forfeit cherished belongings such as clothes, furnishings, books; to be a public nuisance in restaurants where non-smokers endeavour to dine, and on public streets where my cigarette butts add to city debris – the removal of which to be financed by escalating tax burdens assessed to me annually.

I agreed to spending thousands and thousands of pounds to support this most cannibalising habit – taking into account maintenance charges as well as the cost of cigarettes (cigars, pipes, tobacco).

I willingly submitted myself to all manner of personal indignities: being made to feel uncomfortable at meetings, lectures, movies, shows, and all such public places where smoking is forbidden; to sift through the kitchen rubbish to retrieve unextinguished butts; to suffer the panic – having just left home – of hearing a fire engine wailing down my street; to be made to feel inferior by non-smokers; to be made to feel like a hypocrite when I advised my youngsters to eschew all manner of tobacco and never elect to smoke; to suffer the loss of self respect; to sustain deep-seated guilt; to be old before my time; to experience the terror of losing my breath, and putting my very life on the line!

I HEREBY DECLARE THIS SMOKER'S CONTRACT TO BE CANCELLED, REVOKED, DISSOLVED AND RENDERED NULL AND VOID!

(Signed) ____

YOUR NAME

Witnessed this day
of 19

by
(Witnesses Signatures)

RENEWAL CLAUSE

....

THIS IS THE PROVERBIAL DOTTED LINE.

WARNING!
To light but one cigarette, cigar or pipe will be the valid equivalent of rendering my legal signature on this dotted line, renewing the obligation of all aforementioned burdens and humiliations as detailed in the small print aforestated, and to suffer once again the indignities of an existence as an enslaved smoker, with all exigencies herein.

NOTEBOOK PAGES

I WILL STOP SMOKING ON ....

KEY IDEAS AND SESSION NOTES

DIARY

MAJOR LISTS

ASSETS/PERSONAL QUALITIES

DREAMS/GOALS/AMBITIONS/

REASONS WHY I WANT TO STOP SMOKING

A Message from the Author

WHY NOT HELP YOURSELF STOP SMOKING – BY HELPING OTHERS?

Being sponsored by your friends and colleagues to stay off cigarettes could well give you that extra bit of incentive to succeed. You'll be helping others by helping yourself.

You can start the ball rolling by putting aside a portion of the money you'll be saving by not buying cigarettes anymore.

On the reverse of this page is a sponsorship form pledging money to the Imperial Cancer Research Fund, Europe's largest privately financed cancer research institute. Started in 1902, the ICRF was the first institution set up specifically to investigate cancer, its causes and treatment.

With no State or official grants, ICRF carries out about a third of all cancer research in Britain, thanks entirely to the generous support of the public.

While you are, of course, free to give to any charity you want to, I would recommend the ICRF as an extremely appropriate charity in this instance.

And ICRF know the *HabitBreaker* course works. They've already held one of our courses for some of their staff who wanted to stop smoking.

IN SUPPORT OF
THE IMPERIAL CANCER RESEARCH FUND
A SPONSORED STOPPING SMOKING
ENTRY FORM

Your name here ....
I pledge to give ....
(some portion of your savings on cigarettes) to ICRF

The following have also supported me in doing so:

SPONSOR'S NAME AND ADDRESS	Amount per month (up to 3 months)	Total amount pledged	SPONSOR'S SIGNATURE

Signature of participant ....

Date you stopped smoking ....

D		D		D		D		D		D		D		RECAP	
5		5		5		5		5		5		5		5	
6		6		6		6		6		6		6		6	
7		7		7		7		7		7		7		7	
8		8		8		8		8		8		8		8	
9		9		9		9		9		9		9		9	
10		10		10		10		10		10		10		10	
11		11		11		11		11		11		11		11	
12		12		12		12		12		12		12		12	
1		1		1		1		1		1		1		1	
2		2		2		2		2		2		2		2	
3		3		3		3		3		3		3		3	
4		4		4		4		4		4		4		4	
5		5		5		5		5		5		5		5	
6		6		6		6		6		6		6		6	
7		7		7		7		7		7		7		7	
8		8		8		8		8		8		8		8	
9		9		9		9		9		9		9		9	
10		10		10		10		10		10		10		10	
11		11		11		11		11		11		11		11	
12		12		12		12		12		12		12		12	
1		1		1		1		1		1		1		1	
2		2		2		2		2		2		2		2	
3		3		3		3		3		3		3		3	
4		4		4		4		4		4		4		4	
T		T		T		T		T		T		T		T	

MOST SPECIAL THANK YOUs TO:

MIKE FRANKLIN AND CHRIS QUAYLE.

VAL MORGAN (Mother!), KAREN LANGDEN, IAN PROSSER, DAVID MIRANDA, GILLIAN EDWARDS, ANGELA NEWMARCH and JENNY WELLINGTON.

JOHN BROWN, SUE WALLIKER, ONDINE UPTON and MATTHEW FREUD.

MICHAEL KAUDER, TONY MORGAN, MICHAEL WOLFF, PHILIP WILSON, RICHARD SANTONI and DOUG MAXWELL.

NAN BEECHER MOORE, DAN FAUCI, WERNER ERHARD AND HOBIE ALTER.

FIONA FARR, PATRICK HOLFORD, TONI DE KASSEL and UNCLE TOM COBLEY.

And to everyone that's either taken or supported the *Habit-Breaker* courses.

One final acknowledgement to Jacqueline Rogers, a woman whom I have yet to meet but without whom this book would probably not have been written. Mrs Rogers pioneered the research that led to the existence of the *HabitBreaker* courses and, as such, was instrumental in my succeeding at stopping smoking.

FOR FURTHER INFORMATION ON THE HABITBREAKER COURSES

Please call the *HabitBreaker* office on 01 580 5816